Praise for *When Life Hurts:*

"After surviving and coming to terms with his own devastating brush with disaster, Wayne Dosick now teaches others how to overcome life's tragedies and gain strength in the process. *When Life Hurts* offers comfort and hope to anyone who has been touched by life's adversities."

—John Gray, author of *Men Are from Mars, Women Are from Venus*

"Rabbi Dosick shares a practical, powerful true-life story for anyone who has suffered a devastating loss. You will feel deeply moved by the fiery path he and his family were launched upon. More, you will gain the spiritual depth to transform a crisis of the soul into, yes, first breakdown, but then breakthrough. As Rabbi Dosick teaches so eloquently, 'it is you who make your destiny.'"

—Harold H. Bloomfield, M.D., author of
How to Survive the Loss of a Love

"Wayne Dosick has given us a volume of readable, heartfelt inspiration. From his own catastrophe, Rabbi Dosick has coaxed lessons for us all."

—Rabbi David Wolpe, Sinai Temple, Los Angeles;
author of *The Healer of Shattered Hearts*

"A sensitive expression of the profound emotional and interpersonal challenges faced when 'life isn't fair.' *When Life Hurts* offers compassion, understanding, and hope when normalcy and happiness seem too far out of reach."

—Dr. Laura Schlessinger, author of *The Ten Stupid Things
Women Do to Mess Up Their Lives* and *How Could You Do That?!*

"Here is an honest, useful, encouraging, and wise narrative reminding us that adversity may also offer hidden blessings—a chance to reexamine our lives and search for our souls. A thought-provoking read for anyone who has felt the impact of sudden change or loss."

—Dan Millman, author of *Way of the Peaceful Warrior*
and *Everyday Enlightenment*

"Like the biblical psalmist of old, Rabbi Dosick brings comfort and hope to those touched by pain and suffering and offers the assurance that through deep and abiding faith, our mourning will be turned into dancing. *When Life Hurts* is a wise and inspiring book that should be read by every man and woman who wants to be a triumphant survivor."

—Dr. Robert H. Schuller, The Crystal Cathedral;
author of *If It's Going to Be, It's Up to Me*

"Dosick understands that while pain is an inevitable part of life, we can choose to reject misery. Reject it he does—through hopeful parables and a trusting faith. He reminds us that out of dire tragedy can come good, a lesson Oklahomans learned in the wake of the terrible 1995 bombing. In Wayne Dosick's view of life, we are all afloat on God's river, bound in one direction, but it's up to us to handle the oars. Read this book and start rowing!"

—Frank Keating, Governor of Oklahoma

"Rabbi Wayne Dosick's book is a wonderful reflection on living with tragedy, loss, and pain. Speaking from his own experience and out of the riches of his own tradition, he addresses all people of faith. The book is rich in hope, enlivened by the stories the rabbi tells so well, and full of the mystery of God's presence. I recommend it highly."

—Cardinal Roger Mahony, Archbishop of Los Angeles

"Life is a labor pain . . . [but] the pain may lead to enlightenment. . . . Read this book, learn [its] lessons."

—Bernie Siegel, M.D., author of *Love, Medicine, and Miracles*

"Sooner or later the truth of the bumper sticker comes home to everyone: *stuff happens*. What then? How shall we respond? Wayne Dosick is a wise guide who sees patterns and meaning in suffering and tragedy. He knows that adversity paves the way for wisdom and growth. Highly recommended."

—Larry Dossey, M.D., author of
Healing Words and *Be Careful What You Pray For*

"Rabbi Wayne Dosick shows, in a very practical way, how having faith in our essential spirituality can guide and inspire us through some of the most difficult periods of our life. I highly recommend this book."

—Deepak Chopra, author of *The Seven Spiritual Laws of Success*

WHEN
LIFE
HURTS

WHEN
LIFE
HURTS

A Book of Hope

WAYNE DOSICK

HarperSanFrancisco
A Division of HarperCollins*Publishers*

Permissions appear on page 191 and constitute a continuation of this copyright page.

HarperSanFrancisco and the author, in association with The Basic Foundation, a not-for-profit organization whose primary mission is reforestation, will facilitate the planting of two trees for every one tree used in the manufacture of this book.

A TREE CLAUSE BOOK

HarperCollins Web Site: http://www.harpercollins.com
HarperCollins®, ♨ ®, and HarperSanFrancisco™ are trademarks of HarperCollins Publishers Inc.

Book design by Martha Blegen

FIRST EDITION

Library of Congress Cataloging-in-Publication Data
Dosick, Wayne D.
When life hurts : a book of hope / Wayne Dosick.
    p.   cm.
ISBN 0–06–251527–6 (cloth)
ISBN 0–06–251528–4 (pbk.)
1. Providence and government of God—Judaism.   2. Suffering—Religious aspects—Judaism.   3. Disasters—Religious aspects—Judaism.   4. Dosick, Wayne D.   5. Rabbis—California—San Diego—Biography.   I. Title.
BM645.P7D67 1998
296.3'118—dc21   97–33152

98 99 00 01 02 ❖ RRDH 10 9 8 7 6 5 4 3 2 1

For
Ellen

". . . we have endured fire . . .
and God has brought us through . . ."

after Psalms 66:12

שלי ושלכם שלה
Sh'lee v'sh'lachem sh'lah
"Everything that I am,
anything that you may learn from me,
is all thanks to her."

Rabbi Akiba in BT Ketubot 63a

CONTENTS

The message
of God
appeared to them
from out of the flame of fire

after Exodus 3:2

1

FIRE!

I knew that something was very wrong when I saw her standing at the airport gate.

It was almost midnight on October 21, 1996—a date that is now etched into my memory forever. Ellen and I were returning home to San Diego from Chicago after attending the bar mitzvah of my oldest friend's son. We were tired but happy—that kind of deep happiness that comes from having witnessed a meaningful event and from having shared good and sweet time with old and dear friends.

The business at hand now was to collect our luggage, get the shuttle to the parking lot, and drive the forty-five minutes up the coast to our suburban Carlsbad home.

But Karen was standing at the gate.

Karen is my wife's assistant, our sometime houseguest, and, this weekend while we were away, our house sitter. While we were gone, she was to feed the dog and cat, take in the mail and the papers, water the plants, and keep an eye on the house.

There was absolutely no reason that she should be standing at the airport gate at midnight.

We looked at her with, I am sure, a mixture of expectation and fear. She was composed, but her voice was shaking when she said, "There's a fierce Santa Ana [that hot dry wind that now and then whips across Southern California from the desert toward the ocean], and there's a fire in the canyon [that beautiful canyon directly across the street from our house]. At about six o'clock, we were evacuated. I had less than fifteen minutes to get out. I took the dog and the cat, the Torah Scroll, the hard drives from your computers, and a few things off the walls and the shelves. But that's all I could get. By the time I left, the fire was coming right through the canyon. That's all I know. The police have blockaded the street and won't let me back; the news reports keep mentioning the name of your street but don't give any details. I really don't know what has happened to the house."

We listened to her words, but I don't think we comprehended their meaning. What was she saying? What was she saying? Our dog and cat were safe from some danger; our precious Torah Scroll (the Five Books of Moses handwritten in Hebrew on parchment) was safe too. That I understood. But safe from what? Did the fire come out of the canyon into our neighborhood? What was she saying? Had our house burned down?

Bad things happen. Bad things happen that require being personally told at an airport gate. Husbands and wives are in accidents. Children get sick and get hurt and fall in harm's way. Parents suddenly die.

Somewhere in the deep recesses of our minds, we know that danger and disaster are always lurking, and, though we dread it, we know that one day it will be our turn to be told of untimely tragedy. But our house burning down? Even in a region that is known for wildfires, the possibility never entered my mind. Who would ever imagine that beautiful houses on tree-lined suburban streets would burn down? Something like that just doesn't happen. Something like that just doesn't happen to *us*—or so I thought.

Stunned by what Karen had told us, we went to get our suitcases. We stood waiting in silence. There wasn't anything to say. Speculation was fruitless; it was too real to deny, and it was too unfathomable to grasp.

Karen drove us to the lot where we had parked the car. As we paid the parking fee, the attendant said, "Boy, it's really something about those fires up there in Carlsbad." I replied, "We just got off a plane, and we just heard about it. That's where we live. We are going there right now to see if we have a house." He shook his head sadly and said, "I'm prayin' for you, man."

Now, I am a praying man. I am a rabbi who has led congregations in prayer for almost three decades. I am a man of faith who has a personal, intimate relationship with God. But on that ride up the highway—knowing that the parking lot attendant was praying for me—I had trouble praying.

For what should I pray? Should I pray that the fire did not get to my house? With sardonic irony, I remembered the passage from the Mishnah—the 2,000-year-old compendium of Jewish law—that teaches that if a person hears the fire bells in his town, he cannot pray that the fire is not in his house. Why? Because the ringing of the fire bells means that the fire has already started, and even with the most fervent prayer, it is too late; God cannot change reality. Should I pray to God to spare Ellen and me anguish and pain, especially since we are pretty decent people and don't deserve to be hurt in this way? Again, the fire had already come, and if our house had been destroyed, it was too late to do anything about it now. And besides, who ever promised a life without pain and anguish— even for good people?

So, I prayed, as best I could, for the wisdom and the strength to face whatever lay before me—to feel true gratitude and deep joy if our house had been spared; to act with courage and dignity if our house were gone.

We turned on the car radio, but the news reports were of little help. Our neighborhood was mentioned over and over again, and our street too. But there were no details, no specifics. We drove on, still dazed, still frightened, still not knowing.

As we came closer and closer to our highway exit, even in the dark of midnight, we could see the black clouds of smoke, and our nostrils began to fill with the stench of burning. The night air was alive with the sights and the smells of fire. There was no doubt; there had been a great firestorm here. The only question was, Where? Where?

As we drove toward our street, which is about four miles east of the highway, everything looked normal. The houses and stores were there, just as they had been when we left four days earlier. But now an eerie silence enveloped us. It felt, somehow, like the calm *after* the storm, like the interminable moment of vast, breathless quiet that seems to stretch from one end of the universe to the other in the most uncommon and surrealistic of times.

As we came to our street, the twirling lights of fire engines and police cars lit up the night sky. A police officer blocked the way, asking for identification. I knew that he would tell me nothing of what had happened, so I didn't even bother to ask. We drove up the long street. Water poured down the gutter, but the houses seemed all intact. We came to the curve in the street; our house is the second past the curve. I glanced to the left, to the huge canyon. Even in the darkness, I could see that it was blackened and smoldering. We rounded the curve, and I saw the hillside slope of my neighbor's home. It was black; the trees were gone. I said to Ellen, "It doesn't look good."

We made the final turn on the curve, and there it was. Our house and everything in it had burned to the ground. All that was left was the chimney and a part of one wall. Pockets of flame still burned in the ashes.

I don't remember getting out of the car, but somehow I found myself standing in front of what, just hours before, had been our home. One part of me immediately accepted the reality: fires happen, and this fire had happened to us. The other part of me stared in utter disbelief. I don't know where it came from—it must have been from that place in the deepest of the deep inside me—but all of a sudden I heard myself wailing, a deep animal cry of pain and agony. Ellen was weeping softly. She kept saying, "I can't believe it. I can't believe it. Our beautiful house. Our beautiful house. Our beautiful house." I thought that my heart was going to split apart. I began to sob.

After a few minutes, reality began to set in. Our house was gone. All our possessions were gone. All our priceless pictures and memorabilia were gone. All our history was gone.

But, more. For us, this was a double loss. We both worked at home. In our lovely, light-filled house, Ellen, who is a spiritual psychotherapist, saw her clients. I wrote my books and graded my students' papers. Our colleagues and co-workers gathered there. Members of my prayer group came to worship; Ellen conducted her seminars and workshops.

The fire had destroyed not only all our personal belongings, but all the "tools of our trades," all the accouterments and all the records of our professions and our professional lives. We had nowhere to live; we had nowhere to work. We had nothing left in the world except the clothes from the weekend that were in our suitcases in the car.

I don't know how long we stood there. It was really too dark to see very much, and the still-burning embers made it too hot to get any closer. We did the only thing we could do—we held each other and wept. But, eventually, there were things we had to do. We had to find Karen in the supermarket parking lot where we had told her that we would meet. We had to call our parents, who had, undoubtedly, heard about the fire from the media and were, surely, worrying and wondering. We had to find a place to sleep.

My parents immediately invited us to stay with them. The drive to their place on the other side of town took about forty minutes. We drove in stunned silence, punctuated by our tears, by our frequent utterances, "I just can't believe it," and, soon, by our antiphonal litany of all that we had lost.

In my daze, I remembered a story told of the holy Baal Shem Tov, the eighteenth-century rabbi who was the founder of Chasidism, the modern mystical movement of Judaism. One night on Simchat Torah—the holiday when we complete the annual reading of the entire Five Books of Moses by chanting the concluding words of Deuteronomy and immediately begin again with the first words of Genesis—the holy Baal Shem was celebrating by dancing and dancing with the Torah Scroll.

Then, he set aside the Torah Scroll, but he continued to dance.

One of his disciples said to the other, "Our master has set aside the Torah Scroll. Why does he continue to dance?"

The other disciple replied, "Our master has set aside the physical dimension. But the spiritual dimension he has taken inside himself."

I reminded Ellen of the story, and I said to her, "Through no choice of our own, all the things of our physical dimension have been taken away from us in an instant. Maybe, some day, like the Baal Shem, we will be able to take the spiritual dimension inside and continue to dance with God."

I said those words, and I guess—I hope—that I meant them. But I really didn't believe them. I knew that I must be in shock, a shock so deep that I was trying to be rational in the face of overwhelming grief. All I could feel was the agony of loss. I was in almost unbearable pain, and, almost immediately, a deep, deep sadness enveloped me that I knew would last for a long, long time.

Bad Things Happen

I do not mean to be overly dramatic. I do not mean to suggest that a house burning down is the worst thing that could ever happen to a human being. In many ways we were fortunate. We are alive; we are not hurt; even the animals were saved. We were fairly well insured, so the insurance company wrote a check for our immediate needs, rented us a place to live, and told us they would pay to rebuild our house and reimburse us for some of what we lost.

I know that the fire is not the worst thing that could ever happen to me, because I have had other wrenching trauma and pain in my life: I had an infant brother who died, and, although I was too young to know or even remember him, his short life and early death had a profound effect on our family. I had a sweet young wife who died in the early days of our marriage. I have had my share of professional frustration and disappointment, and, like many in highly public positions, I have been subject to wide criticism and malicious gossip. My second marriage failed, and I was divorced from the mother of my children.

And you, too, have had trauma and pain in your life: illness, accident, professional setback, loss of job, financial hardship, bankruptcy, divorce, betrayal by friends; you may have been the victim of mugging, robbery, violence, rape, wounds of war; you may have been battered by hurricane, tornado, earthquake, flood; you may have met with defeat, rejection, humiliation, violation of trust, breach of faith; you may have been discriminated against, isolated, shut out from places you want and deserve to be; you may have agonized over children gone astray; you may have suffered through the illnesses and deaths of your mother, your father, your husband, your wife, your sister, your brother, your son, your daughter, your closest and dearest friends, your cherished pet; you may have endured physical pain and emotional anguish. Your heart may have been broken, and your spirit may have been crushed. You may have felt bitter disappointment and experienced abject failure. You may have gone through incredible loss and been ripped apart by searing grief.

You and I have been struck by the randomness of life and have wondered, "Why me?" You and I have felt the seeming futility of life and have asked, "What did I ever do to deserve this?" You and I have experienced the seeming injustice of life and have cried out, "How could God let this happen?"

The fire was not the worst thing that has ever happened. Yet there is no hierarchy to pain. We cannot measure this loss against that one, this pain against another one. In the midst of our personal agony, we feel the depth of pain that can be compared to no other. Shakespeare understood it best when he said, "And worse I may be yet: the worst is not, / So long as we can say, 'This is the worst.'"

So no matter what pain you and I have already experienced in life, or what pain we may yet experience, the fire can serve as a paradigm for me—and I hope for you—of all the pain and the anguish that life sends our way.

In its shadow, we can ask ourselves, When life hurts so much, how can we cope, how can we hope to struggle through? How can we keep our most intimate relationships whole and healthy? How can our family and friends best serve us when we are in need, and how can we be good friends when others need us? How can we keep our faith in a supposedly just God when life seems so unfair? How can we continue to believe in a God who supposedly watches over us and protects us when so much pain has come our way? How can we affirm a God who supposedly loves us when we feel so bereft and forsaken? Where is God when we need God most? How can we pick up the broken pieces of our lives and make them—and us—whole again?

We Are There Together

I write out of neither time nor perspective. I did not want to "get through" this ordeal and then offer "words of wisdom" either from out of the time that supposedly heals or out of the perspective that supposedly comes with long experience.

I write only a few months after the fire—from out of the bewilderment and the anger and the pain that Ellen and I still feel every day.

Perhaps it would have been wiser to wait. But in the midst of the pain that you may be experiencing right now, or the pain that is still so fresh that you remember it vividly, or the pain that you know is right around the corner because life is like that, I want you to know that you have a friend, you have a companion, who understands. I cannot experience your personal pain, and I would not be so audacious as to say that I know exactly how you feel. But not only have I been there, I am there now.

I can share with you some of my feelings, some of my experiences, some of my understanding of "where you—and I—are at." If I cannot completely empathize by crawling inside you, I invite you to crawl inside me and see me open and wounded. Perhaps you can see some of yourself in me and in what I am going through. And perhaps it can help you face your own trauma, your own monsters, your own pain, knowing that there is someone else who—even though it is for different reasons—hurts the way you do, has to struggle through the way you do, and who eventually will emerge on the other side of pain the way you will.

It is a journey from hurt to healing that we can take together if we both are willing to acknowledge our aching hearts, if we both have the courage to risk confronting the pain in order to find reconciliation and restoration, if we both have the determination not merely to endure but to prevail.

From being battered and broken we *can* become whole and healthy—and happy—once again.

To Guide Us

Two old stories help guide us.

In the last century, a tourist from America visited the famous Polish rabbi the Chofetz Chaim.

The tourist was amazed to see that the rabbi's home was only a simple room filled with books. The only furniture was a narrow bed, a small table, and one straight-backed chair.

"Rabbi, where is your furniture?" asked the tourist.

The Chofetz Chaim looked at him and asked, "Where is yours?"

"Mine? But I am only a visitor here."

Said the rabbi, "So am I."

The second story.

One night, a great sage was disturbed at his prayers by the croaking of a bullfrog. He tried to disregard the unwelcome sound, but to no avail. Finally he shouted out the window, "Quiet. I am at my prayers."

Now this sage was one of the world's great men, so his command was instantly obeyed. Not only the frogs in the vicinity, but every bullfrog in the universe held its voice so that, in the silence, the sage could pray.

But now, another sound intruded on the sage's prayers—an inner voice that said, "Maybe God is as pleased with the croaking of the frog as with the chanting of your prayers."

The sage laughed. "What could possibly please God in the croak of the bullfrog?"

The voice answered, "Why, then, would God have created the sound of the frog?"

The sage decided to find out. He leaned out his window and shouted, "Sing!"

The bullfrog's croaking filled the air, and, soon, all the frogs in the whole world joined in. A chorus of bullfrog croaking filled the universe.

And the sage listened to the sound; he listened very, very carefully. And soon he discovered that if he stopped resisting, if he stopped complaining, the voice of the bullfrog actually enriched the silence of the night.

And the sage's heart became one with the whole universe.

2

YOUR LIFE WILL
NEVER BE THE SAME

We tried to sleep, but, of course, we couldn't. We just held each other and wept. Every time we remembered another treasured possession that we had lost, our hearts broke a little more.

It wasn't quite dawn when we drove—still dressed in the clothes we had been wearing the day before—to what just yesterday had been our home. It was a surreal ride, because all around us, everything looked completely normal. Here were people going to work; here were stores opening for business; here were folks drinking their morning coffee and choosing between a chocolate doughnut or a poppy seed bagel. But for us, nothing—absolutely nothing—was normal.

I remembered what a doctor-friend had told me long ago. He is a pediatric oncologist who is the one who has to tell a mother and father that their beloved child has cancer. In this heart-wrenching session, he always says, "I want you to know that no matter what the outcome—and we have every hope for a very good outcome, because we have great success in treating cases such as this—but no matter what the outcome, from this day on, your life will never be the same. It will always be divided between 'before the diagnosis' and 'after the diagnosis.'"

As we turned the corner to our block, I sensed that my doctor-friend's maxim applied to us too. Our lives will now and forever be defined as "before the fire" and "after the fire."

As we drove up the hill, we were enveloped in the deepest and most eerie silence I have ever experienced. Everything was utterly still; it was almost as if the entire world had stopped breathing. We were hovering, suspended in time, where, for one last second, we might delude ourselves into thinking that this was all a horrible dream.

But as we rounded the curve in the street, any delusions that we still might have held were smacked by reality. It was "after the fire."

Our beautiful home and everything we owned lay in still-smoldering ashes. The entire neighborhood was utterly devastated. It looked like the pictures that I had seen of Hiroshima after the war. Everything—everything—was burned and blackened. A few remnants of chimneys stood mute vigil over the destruction. Burned-out hulls of cars littered the street. What had been stately green trees and lush tropical foliage were now grotesquely charred, twisted slivers of stiffened, dead wood.

My mind echoed the opening words of the biblical book of Lamentations, the eyewitness account of the destruction of ancient Jerusalem and the Holy Temple. "Alas! Lonely sits the city that was once great with people. She has become like a widow. . . . Her gates are deserted . . . Her splendor is gone . . . Jerusalem remembers . . . all the precious things that she once had . . . now, in her downfall, there is none to help her. . . . Bitterly she weeps in the night; her cheeks wet with tears; and there is no one to comfort her" (Lamentations 1:1, 4, 6, 7, 2).

And I knew that my doctor-friend's forewarning to his patients could now be spoken to Ellen and me: "Your life will never be the same."

Meeting with Our Neighbors

Usually we said good morning to one another while we were picking up the morning newspaper from the driveway, or taking the dogs for walks, or getting in our cars to go off to work. On this quiet morning, we neighbors met as we came to begin sifting through the ashes of our lives.

The news reports were in: the fire—now being called by the media the Harmony Grove fire, in order to distinguish our little place in the universe—had completely destroyed more than one hundred homes. Another one hundred homes were so damaged that they were uninhabitable. In our little section of the neighborhood alone, more than thirty houses had been destroyed. The firestorm had roared out of the canyon, jumped the street, and leaped up onto the roofs of our houses. It had raced through our backyards and up the hill to the cul-de-sac behind us. The eight houses on our block and almost every house in the upper cul-de-sac were gone.

But a roaring fire has no discernible pattern and, certainly, no conscience. We understood why the houses with fireproof roofs had survived the blaze, but we could not fathom why one house remained standing between two that were destroyed, or why one house burned down between two that were left completely untouched. We could only stand in awe at the power of the fire and in amazement at its capriciousness.

As we feebly tried to grasp the immensity of the devastation, this little band of neighbors huddled together in shock and pain. Originally, we were bound only by the coincidence of having purchased houses in the same place and, eventually, by some shared experiences and cordial friendships. Now, we are forever linked by our common tragedy. Together, we are known as the "victims" of the Harmony Grove fire. In the early morning light, we hugged, we cried together, and we listened to one another try to make some sense—any sense—out of what had happened. But we could not comfort one another very much, for even with all that we shared, each of us was alone with individual loss.

Our next-door neighbors have a three-year-old daughter and a nursing baby. They had to make immediate arrangements for the health and welfare of their little ones.

Our neighbors on the other side had lived in their house for eighteen years. They had to call their children who are away at college and tell them that their childhood home is gone. In a few months, their daughter is to be married. The woman sobbed, "Now I don't have even one piece of jewelry, not even one cherished keepsake, to pass on to my daughter on her wedding day."

Our back-fence neighbor is an elderly man who takes heart medication. We all worried about whether he had his pills.

In the cul-de-sac lived a family whose thirteen-year-old son was to be bar mitzvah in but three weeks. Everything that had been prepared for this holy occasion—including the prayer shawl that he was to wear, which his grandparents had brought from Jerusalem—had gone up in flames.

The neighbors from the corner house had barely escaped with their lives as they ran from the advancing flames. They were safe, but their precious dogs and cats had perished. Their grief was almost too much to bear.

Our private musings and our collective grieving were not to last long. As the sun rose, the quiet was shattered by the news helicopters flying overhead and the appearance of Red Cross volunteers, insurance company disaster teams, members of the media, local politicians, and the gawkers.

The governor of the state of California came to inspect the damage and to declare our neighborhood a "disaster area." He was quickly followed by the United States secretary of the interior, who said that he would immediately return to Washington to ask the president to offer federal assistance. We were engulfed by those who wanted to help—and by those who wanted to stare. Before long, we felt like animals in a zoo, being examined, exclaimed over, and analyzed by every passerby.

But, in a few hours, the politicians went back to their politics, and the reporters left to file their stories. We were finally left alone to begin sifting through the ashes of our lives.

Loss

Friends brought work gloves, rakes, hoes, and shovels, and we began to slowly dig through the ashes to see if anything—anything at all—had survived. We really did not expect to find anything, for the fire had been so hot—more than 2,000 degrees, we were told—that almost everything had literally vaporized. The destruction was total. We had lost everything.

And how precious were the things that we lost!

Burned up in the fire were all our books, all our papers, all our financial records, all our legal documents; a 6,000-volume rabbinic library, including rare and historic books that are completely irreplaceable; every sermon I had ever written; every note from every class Ellen and I had ever taught; all of Ellen's client records; the tapes of the radio shows I had hosted; Ellen's collection of first-edition books; our childhood teddy bears.

All the keepsakes of a lifetime, all the records and all the memorabilia that were our history and that would help shape our destiny, disappeared in puffs of smoke, and we long for those touchstones reminding us of who we were, what we have become, and what we still might be.

Burned up in the fire was my rabbinic diploma.

I do not need a piece of paper to hang on a wall to prove that I am a rabbi, but my rabbinic diploma was hand-signed by my rabbis and teachers. And more than a third of them— my rebbes and mentors—are now dead. I know that their teachings and their legacies live on in me, but I miss the visible sign of their confidence in me that their signatures represented. And burned up, too, was the picture of my own rebbe, Rabbi Dr. Jakob J. Petuchowski, who has now gone to the Great Beyond. On the eve of my ordination, he inscribed that picture to me with deeply moving words of inspiration and challenge.

Every day, I hear his voice echoing, but I will miss his visage and his handwritten message staring at me from the wall, always calling me to be my best and to do my best.

Burned up in the fire were all our pictures—pictures from grammar school and high school and college; pictures of our childhoods, our birthdays, our bar and bat mitzvahs, our graduations; pictures of camp, of youth groups, of long-ago

(and sometimes long-forgotten) events; pictures of our grandparents, our great-grandparents long dead; pictures of our parents, our sisters, our cousins, our friends; pictures of my
children from the moment they were born, and of how they
grew, and of each milestone in their lives; pictures of our wedding, of our parents' weddings, and my parents' fiftieth wedding anniversary party; pictures of all the places we have
traveled, the sights we have seen, the people we have met; pictures of my Little League team and of Boys' Choir; pictures
taken with the famous and the near-famous—with Mayor
Daley, and with Golda Meir, and with Israeli president
Ephraim Katzir, and with Governor Pete Wilson; a picture of
me standing before Congress when I offered the prayer in the
House of Representatives; Ellen's pictures with her college
roommates, and of her Children's Theater productions, and of
her friends and colleagues all around the country; the enor-
mous number of slides we took on trips to Israel.

All the pictures that were our precious records and cherished memories are gone, and we are left to hope that our all-
too-frail human recall will be sufficient to remind us of the
times and the places of our lives.

Burned up in the fire were Ellen's aunt's gold watch; my
grandfather's pocket watch—given to him at his bar mitzvah
more than eighty-five years ago; my other grandfather's *tallis*
(prayer shawl) with its beautiful, intricately designed silver
neckpiece; Ellen's grandmother's Mother's Day ring, engraved
by her loving children; the gold watch my parents gave me on
the day I was ordained, proudly engraved "to our son, the
rabbi"; the pair of candlesticks given to Ellen on her bat
mitzvah, which she used to welcome the Sabbath every
Friday night.

Gone are all the treasured heirlooms of our lives that can never again be passed down from generation to generation.

Burned up in the fire were all the keepsakes from my first wife, Lauren, who died at such an early age: all the pictures of her and of us together; her books with her handwritten margin notes; the records of her many achievements and accomplishments; all the letters that we had written to each other from the time we were teenagers; so many of the personal items that she had used and that I had saved—her purse, her glasses, her daily calendar, pieces of her jewelry, her comb, her lipstick, a T-shirt that still had the faint scent of her perfume, even after all these years—all the cards and notes of tribute and sympathy that I received when she died.

There is no longer one scrap of paper with her handwriting, not one article that she touched, not one material remnant of her existence on this earth. It feels as if she has died a second time.

Burned up in the fire was a 100-year-old Knabe grand piano, a magnificent instrument that had been in Ellen's family since she was a little girl. And burned up in the fire was a collection of baseball memorabilia: a ball signed by Babe Ruth; a chair from the old Comiskey Park; a ball signed by the members of the 1959 Chicago White Sox World Series team; a vintage collection of 1950s and early 1960s baseball cards. And burned up in the fire was a 5-foot-by-4-foot oil painting done in 1910 by the American Impressionist Pauline Palmer. Her works hang in museums and in private collections throughout the world.

We may have been the "owners" of these treasured pieces in this generation, but they really did not belong to us. We were just this generation's trustees of priceless objects of beauty and history that should have graced this world for hundreds of years more. Although our rational minds know better, our hearts cry out that we somehow failed as good stewards, and we know that the world will be a bit darker and sadder for losing what we failed to protect.

Burned up in the fire was a Hebrew Bible that had once been saved from another fire—the fire of the Holocaust. A friend's father, Hans Spear by name, had escaped from Frankfurt early in the war. But his brother, Ya'akov, refused to leave, for he was a rabbi who was tending children in an orphanage, and he would not abandon them. During the war years, Hans, who, by that time, had settled in America, received packages now and then. Others who were able to escape brought him holy books that Ya'akov had asked them to smuggle out. Eventually, there were more than one hundred books saved from Hitler's hell. After the war was over, Hans searched for his brother, but Ya'akov had been murdered along with six million other Jews. Over the years Hans contributed many of the books to libraries and museums, but he kept about twenty volumes as his spiritual inheritance from his brother. When I was ordained, Hans gave me one of these precious books— a Hebrew Bible that he inscribed with the verse from the prophet Zechariah, "Is this not the firebrand saved from the fire?" (Zechariah 3:2).

This venerable and priceless book had survived the fires of the book burnings, set by the people who hated us, and the conflagrations that swept Europe, set by the people who wanted to murder us. Now, in the freedom and comfort of sunny Southern California, it was burned up by the capricious fire that came out of a pastoral canyon.

All Gone

Besides all the special and precious things that were gone forever, we lost the stability and the reliability of our daily existence.

We no longer had any of the simple, practical necessities of everyday life or any of the things that brought us physical comfort or emotional security. We no longer had any of the things that had created our beautiful surroundings or any of the things that, in so many ways, defined our very existence: our furniture, our clothes, our pots and pans and dishes, the art that had hung on our walls.

Suddenly Ellen and I—whose house had been a haven for us and a gathering place for so many—were homeless. Suddenly we, the rabbi and the psychotherapist—who had guided and counseled so many to "hang in and hold on"—were left emotionally adrift without port or anchor in a big, scary world.

We were not alone. Every one of our neighbors had lost every cherished possession. For all of us, everything familiar, everything comfortable, everything certain, about our lives was gone.

For the adults it was devastating; for the children it was utterly frightening and bewildering. We all felt like Alice who fell down the rabbit hole. Our lives were turned upside down, and we were swirling topsy-turvy.

One wise mother helped her children and the other little ones in the neighborhood begin to cope with the loss. She asked friends to bring large pieces of drawing paper and crayons. She had the children draw scenes from the fire, giving them an outlet to express their confusion, their fears, and their hurts. And she had them write messages to the firefighters. One nine-year-old wrote in big red and green letters. "Dear Mr. Fireman. Thank you for trying to save my house. Unfortunately, it burned down."

Grieving

Our losses were surely severe, and our hearts ached.

But the loss of material possessions cannot begin to compare to the searing pain of loss we all feel when a cherished loved one dies, or the loss of privacy and dignity we feel as the victim of violent crime, or the bewilderment and helplessness we feel at the loss of our job and our source of income, or the utter betrayal we feel at the loss of trust.

Psychologists teach that whenever we experience bitter loss—whatever its source, whatever its consequence—our psyches develop certain mechanisms to help us survive in the face of the unspeakable horror, to help us cope with the almost unbearable pain, and to help us struggle through the utter confusion and the dark anguish.

In her classic work *On Death and Dying,* Dr. Elisabeth Kübler-Ross taught that the terminally ill—and, by extension, we who are bereaved and in mourning—go through five stages in the process of grieving.

The first stage is denial—which Ellen and I felt when we stood before the smoldering ashes of our home, and which we all experience when we get the telephone call with the news that a loved one has suddenly died. We keep saying, "I just can't believe it; I just can't believe it. It can't be happening. It's impossible. It can't be real. It's all just a bad dream."

The second stage is anger.

We get mad at the doctor: "Why didn't you work harder to save his life?" We get mad at nurses and at the clergy: "Why didn't you stop in his room more often, visit her one more time? You should have cared more." We get mad at the perpetrator: "How dare you drive drunk? If it weren't for your careless disregard for human life, the accident would never have happened." We get mad at society: "How can this country let these animals roam the streets like this, hurting innocent people?" We get mad at the victim: "What were you doing out so late at night? Didn't you know that it was dangerous and that you could get hurt?" We get mad at the deceased: "How could you die and leave me alone like this?" We get mad at God: "How could You let this happen? How could You do this to me?"

Ellen and I felt this kind of anger as we stared at the ashes and were faced, inexorably, with our devastating loss. "Where was the fire department? How come they saved that house and not ours? How did this fire start? Was it a careless smoker, a transient's campfire in the canyon? Who owns that canyon? Why wasn't the brush cut back? Let's find out and sue for millions of dollars."

We were also angry because we felt so helpless, so impotent.

Faced with loss, all of us feel this lack of control. None of us has the power to ward off the death of our loved ones. Few of us have the power to elude the disease that debilitates. Fewer of us have the power to protect ourselves or one another from brutal assault on body or spirit. Still fewer have the power to protect our children from sudden devastating illness or from predators who stalk the young and innocent.

Ellen and I felt completely powerless. Our ability to control our lives had been ripped away from us.

In our anger, born out of fear and dread, we found our-selves shouting out in pain and in helplessness.

Together and alone, in places like the shower and the car where no one else could hear us, we screamed, and pounded our fists, and railed against our fate.

And we found that shouting was a good outlet, a welcome release, for all our pent-up frustration and anger, for all our feelings of grief and impotence.

The third stage of grieving is bargaining.

We all know how this goes: "God, if You just let my mother live, I'll do whatever You ask of me for the rest of my life." Or, "If I only were a better daughter, my father wouldn't be sick." Or, "Oh God, if You get me out of this mess, I'll give a big contribution to charity, and I'll go to church every Sunday from now on." Or, "What if she had left only two minutes ear-lier, only two minutes later, wouldn't she have avoided the acci-dent?" Or, "What if I hadn't let him take the car tonight, wouldn't he still be alive?"

And, of course, our bargaining and calculating soon begins to take on our own desire to control the situation, our own sense of power and possibility. "If only I had been there, I would have told the doctor what to do." "If only I had been driving, the accident never would have happened." "If only I had been with her, I would have protected her and she would not have been hurt."

For Ellen and me, our bargaining first took the form of a little game that we instinctively began to play that we called "What If?" What if we had been home? What if *we* had had the fifteen minutes to rescue our possessions from the quickly advancing fire? What would we have taken? What would we have saved? What would we still have that is now lost forever?

Soon, our own purported abilities and powers began to take on heroic proportions. "If only we had been there, we would have been able to save everything that was precious."

Of course, we will never know what we might have done or what we might have saved.

We cannot even begin to speculate about how we would have behaved with fire bearing down on us. Perhaps we might have arrogantly assumed that the fire would never make its way to our house. We might have waited too long and, when forced to flee, been able to take absolutely nothing. Perhaps we would have panicked and taken little things that, at the moment, seemed important but later might have seemed like silly choices. Perhaps, in our haste, we might have forgotten some very important things and then chastised ourselves forever. Perhaps we would have taken some more "right" things than Karen, the house sitter, was able to take. But, in the end, would it have made much difference? With almost everything else gone, would having a few more items of material or senti-mental value make us feel any better?

Soon after the fire we received a letter from a friend. She helped us put our sad game of "What If" into perspective when she wrote, "The fact that you weren't home is the prover-bial blessing in disguise. Owning so many precious and valu-able items, you might have misjudged the things you wanted to save and the speed of the firestorm. The house sitter was able to act objectively. God was at your side, keeping you out of that house."

Our friend was right: our bargaining was ultimately futile. But it served its purpose for us, as it does for everyone in a sad or tragic situation, by helping us take one small step toward understanding, acceptance, and healing.

The "Stuff" of Our Lives

But—even with our intellectual understanding of the stages we were going through and the process we were experiencing—everything we owned was still gone, and our hearts hurt, and our sense of loss was overwhelming.

Each and every thing that we lost—from the most precious and priceless to the most mundane and simple—had its own unique place in our lives.

And, now, we have to live without them all.

I remembered that I once gave a sermon entitled "What Shall I Put in My Cardboard Box, and Who May Ride in My Spaceship?" It was a meditation on which people and what things are most important to each of us. In the sermon, I asked myself and my listeners: If I were being sent into outer space on a long journey, and there were room in my spaceship for only a few people, whom would I choose to go with me? And if I were going to leave home for another place, another country, a desert island, and I could take with me only a few precious objects—nothing more than could fit in a standard-sized cardboard box—what would I take?

In this little game of pretend, our choices of people and possessions tell a great deal about our values and our priorities. They go a long way toward answering that age-old question, "Who am I, and what is my life?"

Now, through no choice of our own, Ellen and I were faced with a real-life situation that matched my homiletic game.

Ellen and I had had a lot of "stuff."

Only six or eight weeks before the fire I had said to her, "You know, if anyone ever wanted to offer us jobs somewhere other than San Diego, we would never be able to take them, because no one could afford our moving expenses."

Now, everything we have could fit into my one sermonic cardboard box.

Overnight, we had to begin to define and redefine our relationship to the things—the "stuff" in our lives.

The comedian George Carlin talks about all the "stuff" that we acquire. We get a house, but it is empty, because we do not have any "stuff." So we buy and buy, and pretty soon, we have lots of "stuff." It's not long before we have too much "stuff" to fit in our house, so we buy a bigger house that can hold more "stuff." But, of course, we don't have enough "stuff" to fit in the bigger house, so we go out and buy more and more "stuff." And the cycle of acquiring more "stuff" continues and continues and continues.

The things we owned—the "stuff"—were useful and beautiful and historical and evoked warm memories, but, in the end, they were just things.

We all spend a lot of time and effort working to earn the money to buy things, to acquire material possessions. We need many of these things to make our lives, and the lives of our children, livable and comfortable. We need a place to live and clothes to wear and food to eat; we need the practical necessities of life, and we are glad to have some of the material luxuries that we earn and think that we perhaps deserve.

But a situation such as this caused us to ask ourselves, How many pairs of pants can one person wear? In how many chairs can one person sit? How many cars can one person drive?

How many things do we need to have to be satisfied, to be happy? How many material possessions do we need to acquire to consider ourselves secure? How many fancy brand names do we need to have in our closets, in our driveways, on our

shelves, to consider ourselves successful? How can we let adver-
tisers and public relations press releases and television com-
mercials and celebrity spokespeople define our sense of
self-worth?

The Mishnah, the ancient compendium of Jewish law, asks,
"Who is rich?" The answer is not the one who accumulates
wealth or material possessions. "Who is rich? The one who is
content, who is satisfied, with his, with her, portion in life"
(Avot 4:1).

We asked ourselves: was the fire, somehow, sending us a
message?

Were we being told that we had too many things? Were we
being told that we were too attached to material possessions?
Were we being told that the things we owned burdened us and
weighed us down? Were we being told to reevaluate our relationship to work, to earning money, and, thus, to the things
that money can buy? Were we being told to disencumber our
beings and lighten our lives?

After all, the things we would miss the most, the things that
were most precious to us, had cost the least—photos, keepsakes from childhood, letters from family and friends, inscrip-
tions in books, the Father's Day and birthday cards that my
sons had drawn for me when they were little boys.

So we began to wonder about all the things we owned, all
the material possessions that seemed so valuable, so priceless,
to us. What would have happened to them thirty or forty years
from now when we die?

The items that belong to the generations—the piano, the
painting, the baseball memorabilia—might have gone to collec-
tors or even to museums. Some of the papers and the records
of my rabbinate might have gone to the American Jewish
Archives—not because I am particularly important or famous,

but simply because the Archives collects the work of all rabbis as primary source material of American Jewish history.

But what of all the other things, the precious items that we cherished so much? My children would have taken the three or ten things that had meaning or value to them. Out of nostalgia, obligation, or guilt, they might have kept a few more items that they knew had particular meaning to me. Our nieces and nephews might have taken something "to remember Aunt Ellen and Uncle Wayne." But the rest of all our things would have, most likely, wound up in an estate sale or been given to Goodwill or the Salvation Army. Everything that once meant so much to us would, eventually, have become just another antique, another curiosity, or another item for sale at a thrift shop.

The fire just accelerated the process of dispersion by thirty or forty years.

God Within

Yet we cannot simply consign the things in our lives to being *just* material objects, to being just *things*.

Everything in the universe—human beings and rocks and radishes and houses and oranges and chairs—is created by God. Everything is filled with Divine life force. Everything, every *thing*, is animated by God's light and filled with God's energy.

Scientists may call this the phenomenon of faster- or slower-moving atoms.

I call it God within.

When anyone, when anything, ceases to exist on earth, it is cause for grief and sadness—not just for the survivors who are left bereft, but for the person himself, for the object itself, that gives up temporal existence on earth.

That is why, when our parents die, we feel our own keen sense of loss and longing, and we also are deeply aware of what *they* have lost. They will not be at a grandchild's wedding. They will not meet their great-grandchildren. They will not know who won the presidential election or the World Series.

That is why I feel so bad about all our things that were lost in the fire. I not only feel bad about losing them, but I feel bad for the *things themselves*.

In my mind's eye, I do not see the fire consuming the whole house all at once, but individual flames coming into area after area, room after room, touching item after item, one at a time.

I see the fire coming into my study from the ceiling and making its way down the walls to the floor. The fire did not devour everything at once in one giant whoosh of flame, but—in an almost delicate, slow-motion dance—it engulfed each individual item, one by one. When the ceiling was being consumed, the pictures were still on the walls, and my pens were still on my desk.

In my distress, I wonder: if pictures could talk—which, of course, they cannot—would they have screamed in fear, or would they have remained stoically quiet as the flames advanced down the wall toward them? If pens could talk—which, of course, they cannot—would they have cried out in pain, or would they have remained bravely silent as the flames first licked, and then enveloped, and then consumed them?

Objects may not have feelings as we know them, but objects have being—God-being. It may not be life as we know it, but it is God-given existence.

All the things in our house burned up and are gone, and we mourn their loss—for us and for them, too.

Energy Within

When we lose precious objects, our mourning is intensified because part of our own energy is in those objects.

We had touched, we had used, we had worn, we had held, we had played with, we had caressed, everything we lost. In the touch, in the wearing, in the caress, we had—consciously or unconsciously, decisively or subtly—transferred a portion of our energy onto the object. The rings Ellen wore took on her energy; the baseball mitt I played with took on my energy.

In an instant, along with the object that held it, a portion of our energy left this earth. We lost not only the things, but the part of ourselves that they held.

That is why, in the face of a great loss, particularly when a loved one dies, we all feel so low, so spent, so dispirited, so weak. Not only are we in shock and in pain, not only are we struggling to live without what we have lost, but we are literally diminished in strength and energy, for part of our own energy has left us.

The process of grieving and mourning that we all go through at a time like this is the slow but deliberate reclaiming of our energy.

Tentatively and gingerly, we reach over and gradually take back that part of us that has gone over to another dimension.

It is a difficult and painful process, but once we have reclaimed our own energy, we can gently let go of what is gone. We reanimate and reenergize ourselves, and we take one more small step toward healing and acceptance.

Where Have All Our Things Gone?

What ultimately happened to all our things?

The firefighters said that the fire was so hot that almost everything vaporized; everything just vanished into thin air.

What happens to objects—created and sourced by the spark of God—when they leave this earth, when they seem to have just disappeared into nothingness?

Scientists would say that the atoms continue to exist in another form. Ice becomes water; water becomes the gases of its component elements. Chairs burned up by fire become faster-moving molecules and take on a different molecular structure.

My view is that the energy of the object—the Godliness that is inherent within it—transmutes into a different form of God-energy.

In one form—a chair, a piano, a painting, a teddy bear—God-energy manifests certain characteristics and serves us on this earth in a particular way.

Transmuted, it serves us in a different way.

All that was consumed by the fire returned to its energy source—God. In God, it takes on another form—a form that we can no longer see or touch, but that is as bound up with our being as the chair we sat on or the teddy bear we cuddled.

The energy of all the things that we had on earth now serves us in spirit—in reformulated God-energy—as a guide: to memory, to mourning, to compassion, to loving, to understanding, to renewing, to destiny; as a guide to attaining whatever qualities and capabilities we need in order to learn and grow and become.

Our relationship to our things has certainly changed. But they continue to be with us and to serve us. Their being and their value remain immutable and abiding. It is for us to now see them in their new embodiment and to appreciate them in their transformed and transforming role.

Life's Losses

Someone—by some accounts, a cynic; by other accounts, a pragmatist—once said, "All of life can be summed up in three continually recurring themes: anticipating loss, loss, and grieving over loss."

Though this wry observation of life may be an exaggeration, it contains more than a kernel of truth.

Life is a series of losses.

The writer Judith Viorst described many of them as "necessary losses" and characterized them as "the loves, illusions, dependencies, and impossible expectations that all of us have to give up in order to grow."

We know, for example, that we will lose our childhood deference to grown-up self-reliance; we know that we must lose our youthful innocence to adult confidence; we know that, if the world unfolds in right order, we will lose our parents to old age and death; we know that, in the course of time, we will lose our own vigor and strength to frailty and infirmity.

But there are some losses that are completely unexpected, that upset the natural order, that turn our world upside down, that throw our lives into chaos and confusion. No one expects that his young parent will drop dead. No one expects that she will be raped. No one expects that his best friend will betray him. No one expects that her reputation will be sullied. No one expects his house to burn down. No one expects to be paralyzed by a freak accident. No one expects her child to die.

But all these losses happen because life happens. We lose the things that are most dear to us; we lose the people we most love; we lose control of our physical being; we lose our honor and our good name.

Our losses can break us.

Or, if we can see them in a different perspective, they can serve us.

We can be like the man who was wearing only one shoe.

Someone said to him, "I see that you have lost a shoe."

"No," he replied. "I found one."

Everything that we know best and everyone that we love most is made of God-energy. Though we would be most comfortable and happy having that God-energy in familiar physical form, it can serve us and guide us in any and every form.

When our parents die, when our precious children are taken from us, when our most cherished friends leave this earth, their earth-bound energy returns to God, who gave it, and is transformed into the energy of God-spirit. Our loved ones leave the physical realm, but they never leave us alone in the world of the spirit. Though we may not be able to see them or touch them in our world of temporal reality, they are always here. The words and deeds of a cherished relative or friend can echo across time and remain a powerful presence. The wide grin and tender innocence of a beloved child can bring us timeless delight. The unconditional love and unqualified affirmation of a parent long gone can envelop us and sustain us forever. Even from the Great Beyond, in their God-energy, they love us and they guide us.

As the modern prayer book teaches, "Death is not an end; the earthly body vanishes, but the immortal spirit lives with God" (UPB I).

As Ellen and I slowly began to recognize and accept this hard but deep truth, we took one small step toward understanding and accepting our loss, one more step toward reconciliation and healing.

In the Hand of God

Even as we began sifting through the ashes, looking for any remnants of our devastated home and possessions, we knew that, somehow, God and the universe were looking out for us and taking care of us. For in the ashes, we found amazing little messages.

Here and there were lumps of metal, burned and fused together. To any objective observer, they were just unrecognizable pieces of junk. But to us they were precious, for we knew what they used to be. We found the lump that used to be my grandfather's pocket watch, the lump that used to be the cap of a pen given to me as a gift when I was ordained, the lump that used to be one of Ellen's bracelets. These blackened lumps of metal are totally useless—they will never again tell time or write a letter—and all we can do with them is keep them in a box on a shelf somewhere. But we felt as if the ashes were giving us little touchstones of what we once cherished and little gifts of memory of what we once had.

A few burned and singed pages still remained from the more than 6,000 books that were destroyed. How these few delicate pieces of paper survived the inferno, we will never know. But, clearly, their survival was not just random—they were not simply pages from cookbooks or "beach novels." The few words that were left from the millions and millions that were destroyed contained deep and powerful meaning.

The first page we found was from a book entitled *Twilight,* by the Holocaust survivor and Nobel laureate Elie Wiesel.

Raphael asked him, "And God in all this? Tell me, would God allow it?"

And the old man answered:

"God? Did you say God?" And he burst into laughter.

We cannot identify the source of the next page we found, but it seems also to be from the writings of Elie Wiesel. Most of the page was burned away, but we could read a few words, and we filled in the rest.

I asked him point blank: "How can you believe in Hashem [God] after the Khourban [the Holocaust]?" He looked at me and said, "How can you not believe after the Khourban?"

The remnants were telling us what we already knew: God did not cause the fire; God does not want us to suffer and be in pain. But in our suffering, in our pain, God is with us.

One of our friends who was helping us dig through the ashes excitedly ran over clutching something he had found in the area that had been the garage. It was a piece of what had been a cup made out of glazed pottery that we had used for our Passover celebrations. Still clearly visible on the shard was one Hebrew word that had been emblazoned on the cup אליהו *Eliyahu,* Elijah.

Jewish tradition says that Elijah the prophet is the one who will herald the coming of the messianic age of peace and tranquillity. That is why he is symbolically invited to every Passover *seder*—to move our thoughts and our hearts from the commemoration of the historical redemption from Egyptian slavery to the hope and the promise of ultimate redemption, a world of peace under the Kingdom of God. When we established our prayer group a few years ago—a prayer group that is dedicated to exploring reemerging Jewish spirituality and to helping shape and forge Judaism's coming new age—we named it The Elijah Minyan, invoking the memory of the ancient prophet who will announce the new era of universal harmony.

Of all our religious and ritual objects that might have been saved from the fire, how sweetly ironic it is that the name of Elijah came through unscathed, bringing us the assurance of personal salvation for ourselves and ultimate redemption for our world.

We found three more singed pieces of paper that we could still read.

One piece had only one sentence on an otherwise totally charred page. It said, "Shechinah [the nurturing, sheltering Divine presence] accompanies all of Israel's exiled."

In finding that scrap of paper, we were certain: We may be without a home, but we are never without God. For God will never leave us alone.

We found a page that had blown over into our neighbor's ashes. He brought it over and said, "I think that this is yours." It was the remnant of a brochure for my first book. The edges were completely burned away, but the title of the book was still clearly readable in big letters in the center of the page: *The Best Is Yet to Be.*

With tears in his eyes, my neighbor quietly asked, "Do you think that I could possibly have this?" I handed it to him, and we hugged.

Finally, we found a page that had three Hebrew words on it. They are the words that we recite after we read the final words of each of the five books of the Hebrew Bible during the annual synagogue reading cycle: חזק חזק ונתחזק *chazak, chazak v'netchazak.* "Be strong; be strong. And let us strengthen one another."

In our bewilderment and our pain, the ashes—and the universe—gave us directive and mandate to be strong and to prevail. And we felt a strange sense of hope and assurance.

Now, I am sure that as you read these words, you are saying to yourself, "This just isn't possible. It's too contrived; it's too trite. How could everything have burned up, while these few items—these few pieces of paper with their perfectly appropriate words—survived? It can't be. He's just making it up."

But I'm not making it up. Everything I am telling you is true.

For, you see, nothing happens by chance; there are no coincidences. There is a Divine plan. There is a reason and—even though we do not know it now—an ultimate explanation for what happened to us.

So—even though our hearts were overflowing and our eyes were dimmed with tears, even in our bewilderment and our pain—we stood in the ashes of what, just yesterday, had been our home, and we read the perfect cosmic messages that were being given to us.

And we knew that, eventually, we would be all right.

For we knew that we were being Divinely guided; we knew that we were being held in the gentle hand of God.

3

OF FAMILY AND FRIENDS

Even in tragedy, even in pain, we were incredibly blessed.

Almost immediately, family and friends began to converge on us, in person and by telephone, from every corner of the globe. We no longer had anything but the proverbial "shirt on our back," but we were instantly wrapped in human concern and deepest love. The human community swiftly began to help repair what nature had destroyed.

Within hours our brother-in-law the attorney came to be with us and to help us deal with the insurance company. Our closest friends came to help us dig through the ashes. Our sisters began collecting duplicate pictures from their albums so that we would have some family photos. Our other brother-in-law called his rabbi to ask him to post the news of the fire on the Internet and to ask colleagues and associates to send sacred books to help restore my library. Our parents opened their homes, their hearts, their checkbooks, to provide whatever we needed, because when their children—even their middle-aged children—are hurt, they, too, hurt, and they wanted to do anything and everything they could.

"Your Friend Is Your Needs Answered"

Our family and closest friends enveloped us in comfort and wrapped us in love. It was not so much their words or their deeds, but their very presence—their caring, loving, sheltering presence—that brought us solace. They hugged us when we were bereft; they caught our tears when we wept. They listened and listened and listened as we poured out our hearts and tried to make some sense of our tragedy. They provided steadfastness in a time of chaotic upheaval, a calm assurance that we would eventually emerge from searing pain to renewal and healing.

Deeply moved and constantly overwhelmed by their care, their love, their generosity, I remembered the line from *The Prophet,* by Kahlil Gibran: "Your friend is your needs answered."

How we were in need.

And how our family and our friends were our answer.

Their swift and selfless response to our needs reminded me of a story that I have often told:

"My friend is not back from the battlefield, sir," one soldier said. "Request permission to go out and get him."

"Permission denied," said the officer. "I don't want you to risk your life for a man who is probably dead."

Disobeying orders, the soldier went anyway. An hour later, he returned, carrying the corpse of his friend, but mortally wounded himself.

The officer was filled with grief. "I told you that he was dead," he said. "Now I've lost both of you. Tell me, was it worth going out there to bring in a corpse?"

"Oh, it was, sir," the dying man replied. "You see, when I got to him, he was still alive, and he said to me, 'Jack, I was sure that you would come.'"

Our friends are people like this—devoted, loyal, passionate, compassionate. When we needed them most, they came to us. And in the midst of our shock and our sadness, they lifted our spirits and gave us hope.

When life's troubles come your way, as they inevitably will, I hope that you have—and will open yourself to—friends like these.

An Outpouring of Concern

Our family and our closest friends were not the only ones to immediately respond to our needs. Colleagues, congregants, clients, acquaintances, and total strangers all wanted to help.

Very first on the scene was the Red Cross. I know that it is their "job" to help victims of disaster, but these volunteers went far beyond any requirement or expectation. They truly cared. They continually made sure that we had food and water, that we filled out the applications for federal assistance, that we got the gift certificates and discount coupons offered by local merchants. They sent their staff psychologists to talk and—more important—to listen. They not only met our needs, they anticipated them. The Red Cross really lived up to its mission and to its reputation, and I know that every one of our neighbors is thankful and deeply grateful for the assistance we all received.

A group of ten-and eleven-year-old boys in the neighborhood felt terrible about the houses that had been destroyed and very grateful that their own houses had been spared. They took up a collection of their own money and raised $300, which they took to the local home improvement–hardware store to buy supplies to help all of us dig through our ashes. Hearing what they were doing, the manager of the store immediately matched their money with another $300. Word of this collection quickly spread through the store, and the customers who were shopping at the time opened their own wallets and purses and contributed another $500. The next day, a big truck from the store, with all the young boys aboard, drove through the neighborhood giving out more than $1,100 worth of rakes and shovels, work gloves, garbage bags, and waste buckets—all the equipment we needed to sift the ashes.

A number of women in the neighborhood bought wood and wire screening and, with their own hands, made large sifters—like the ones that are used at archaeological digs. They walked from house to house, giving each family a large and a small screen-sifter that we could use to sift out any tiny precious items that might have been left in the ashes. After their visit, we began calling our house not "the house" or "the ashes," but "the site"—the archaeological site of our home that we were digging and sifting.

A woman I had met once in the local post office came and said, "I hardly know you; we met just once. But I feel so sorry for you. I was evacuated, but, thank God, my house is OK. I want to help you in any way that I can. Put me to work." That woman dug all day—getting filthy from the soot of the ashes and burned from the heat of the sun. At the end of the day, she hugged us and said, "Thank you for letting me help."

A woman walked up to me and handed me a plastic bag filled with ice, two cans of root beer, and two peanut butter cups. She said, "My house burned down in the Oakland Hills fire a few years ago. As I was digging through my ashes, a stranger came up and gave me two cans of root beer and two peanut butter cups. Even in the horror of the moment, it made me smile and feel a little better. I'm a stranger to you, but now I am returning the favor that was once done for me. I am bringing you root beer and peanut butter cups. I hope that they will make you smile and feel a little better." They—and she—did.

A rabbinic colleague called from Tokyo. He had read of the fire on the Internet and wanted us to know that we were in his thoughts and his prayers. Another colleague called from Baltimore to remind me that his rabbinic library had been destroyed by a fire in his synagogue a few years ago. He, of all people, could really understand the utter emptiness I felt at the loss of my precious books, and he, of all people, could best advise me on how to deal with the insurance company about replacement values.

I teach the only courses in Jewish Studies at the University of San Diego, a Catholic university. Right after the fire, my teaching colleagues there took up a collection for us, and the collection at the students' Sunday evening mass at the Founder's Chapel was taken on our behalf. Priest friends from around the county sent us checks from their emergency funds. How sweet was the spirit of ecumenical friendship as the church and its pastors came to the aid of a rabbi in need.

One of Ellen's sisters was to be married in Berkeley in less than two weeks. The bridesmaid dress Ellen was to wear burned up in the fire. Ellen's sister called the dress manufacturer in Massachusetts and explained the situation. The manufacturer worked overtime to make another dress and send it to us in San Diego. With only hours to go before we had to leave, Ellen's seamstress stayed up half the night sewing the alterations. A day later, Ellen—properly and beautifully attired— was a proud bridesmaid at her sister's wedding.

A young woman whom we had never met brought a bouquet of flowers to "the site." She handed them to Ellen, hugged her, and said, "God be with you." Without another word, she left. We have never seen her again.

On the second day after the fire, two firefighters who had been on duty for more than thirty-six hours, first battling the blazes and then dousing the flare-ups, drove up in their own truck. They said. "We are so sorry for your loss. We tried so hard, we did everything that we could, but the fire beat us. Is there anything we can do to help you now?" And for the next two hours, until darkness stopped them, these exhausted, sad but proud men helped us shovel and sift and move the few pieces of remaining steel that were too heavy for us to lift alone.

Within three days of the fire, Ellen had more than a dozen offers of office space in which to conduct her practice. The offers came from colleagues and friends, and from total strangers who had heard or read of our plight.

A friend dropped off a shopping bag at my parents' house, saying, "This is for Ellen and Wayne." In it were a Bible, a prayer book, and a pair of Sabbath candlesticks.

The Greatness of the Human Spirit

People from all over brought and sent us clothes, money, food, books, household utensils, pictures. Rabbinic colleagues sent books, and the members of our prayer group took up a very generous collection to help me restore my library.

We got hundreds and hundreds of phone calls (what an amazing job the telephone company did in forwarding calls to my parents' number, in setting up voice mail, and in replacing cellular phones). We received hundreds and hundreds of letters and cards—all with good wishes, with messages of support and encouragement, with prayers for strength and healing.

Local restaurants offered meals; local shops and national chain stores offered discounts. The local post office set up a special window so that, at our convenience, we could retrieve the mail that was held for us.

The local cable television company—which, in those few hours, had lost more than one hundred customers and all the hardware and equipment that was in our houses—called to express sympathy and to tell us to disregard last month's bill. The local library forgave us the responsibility we had for books out on loan that were destroyed in the fire, and the Friends of the Library Committee immediately began raising the funds to replace what had been lost.

A hundred times, a thousand times, we heard the words, "I want to help. Whatever I can do for you, just let me know."

Every time these words were spoken, they were said with sincerity and with conviction.

In the aftermath of the fire, the human spirit was at its highest and its finest. Individuals banded together for the common good. Family, friends, and strangers reached out to those of us in need with deep-felt concern and with selfless generosity. Expressions of sympathy and comfort were never-ending; acts of genuine kindness were myriad. Love and—when we were ready—sweet laughter filled our empty spaces and helped mend our battered souls.

Frankly, it was hard—very, very hard—for Ellen and me to accept all the kindnesses that were being bestowed on us. We, who had spent our lifetimes as a rabbi and a therapist giving to others, found it very hard to take from others. Perhaps we did not want to admit our helplessness; perhaps we did not want to acknowledge our lack of control over our own lives. Perhaps we were embarrassed at the attention being paid to us or at being at the center of so many people's concern. Whatever the reason, our gratitude for the help we were being given was liberally mixed with our discomfort at needing it—and wanting it.

Yet Ellen and I—and all our neighbors—felt truly fortunate at the outpouring of human affection, truly honored by the beneficence of the human heart, and truly blessed by the goodness and the greatness of the human spirit.

It would be easy to attribute all these many kindnesses to ordinary people reacting in extraordinary ways to uncommon circumstances. Tragedy may have increased visibility and heightened awareness, but I think that what we were witnessing was people—who are by their very nature extraordinary—behaving in their ordinary ways. Even with all the foibles and failings of humanity, most people are inherently decent and good. Most people want to do what is right, and, every day, the work of their hands reflects their commitments. We are God's children, doing God's work on earth by letting God's providence and grace flow through us.

The Debasement of the Human Spirit

But, sad to say, in the aftermath of the fire, we also witnessed the human spirit at its lowest.

Along with those who wanted to help came the ones who just wanted to look. They came in such numbers that the neighborhood was clogged with cars; there was an ongoing traffic jam on our quiet suburban street. They drove by slowly, stopping whenever they could, and looked and pointed and stared. When the police finally put up blockades at the bottom of the hill to keep these "lookie-loos" away, they were not deterred. They parked their cars on other streets, walked up the hill, and stood in front of the house-site, pointing and staring. Rarely did they say anything; never did anyone express sympathy or concern. They just came to point and stare.

Almost immediately, they were joined by the "ambulance chasers," the salespeople and entrepreneurs who wanted to "make a quick buck" from our tragedy. Wrapping themselves in the guise of sympathetic concern, the public insurance adjusters tried to get us to sign up with them—at a mere 30 percent contingency fee—to represent us and our best interests in what they assured us would be dreadful negotiations with our insurance company. The general contractors came to sell their services to rebuild our house, assuring us that their experience and expertise in construction would result in a much better house than the one we had just lost hours before. "Hire me," one said, "and it won't be long before you forget that you ever lived in a house as poorly constructed and as inadequate as this one."

As if dealing with insensitive and boorish people were not enough, we had to consider the possible appearance of malicious people. The insurance company directed us to put up a six-foot-high security fence, topped with barbed wire, all around our property. For, if anyone decided to "explore" our house-site and somehow got hurt, we could be sued for damages. An intruder trespassing on the remains of our destroyed house and injuring himself could sue us. Unbelievable! What a world!

It wasn't long before the human spirit at its lowest proved the fence necessary, but, unfortunately, ineffective. Four or five nights after the fire, someone climbed the fence, cut the barbed wire, and took all the tools that we left on the property each night. The very rakes and hoes and shovels that our friends had brought and that the youngsters in the neighborhood had given us to sift through the ashes were stolen by a thief in the night. The tiny, tiny remnant of all that we owned on our land was now gone too.

What is it in human nature that causes some people to want to see other people's tragedies, to view other people in grief, to watch other people cry? What is it in human nature that causes some people to want to take advantage of other people when they are hurting and most vulnerable, when they are least capable of making sound and thoughtful decisions? What is it in human nature that causes some people to violate other people's boundaries and privacy and dignity? What is it in human nature that causes some people to crush the human spirit rather than to elevate it?

We are a swirl of contradictions.

Of dust we are made, but our breath, our spirit, is the breath and the spirit of God.

The spirit of God was so evident in the many, many people who came in affection and sincerity to share in our grief and to help in our recovery. It was sad that others manifested the dust—the crude, debased elements of our nature—by further exacerbating our pain and preying on our sorrow.

Elevating the Human Spirit

One of my favorite stories reminds us what a saner, happier, more contented world it would be—what a *better* world it would be—if we could all constantly tap into the highest and greatest elements of our nature, if we could all strive to raise up the human spirit and celebrate it.

High in the mountains was a monastery that had once been known throughout the world. Its monks were pious; its students were enthusiastic. The chants from the monastery's chapel deeply touched the hearts of those who came there to meditate and to pray.

But something changed. Fewer and fewer young men came to study there; fewer and fewer people came for spiritual nourishment. The monks who remained became disheartened and sad.

Deeply worried, the abbot of the monastery went off in search of an answer. Why had his monastery fallen on such hard times?

The abbot went to a wise master, and he asked, "Is it because of some sin of ours that our monastery is no longer full of vitality?"

"Yes," replied the master. "It is the sin of ignorance."

"The sin of ignorance?" questioned the abbot. "Of what are we ignorant?"

The wise master looked at the abbot for a long time, and then he said, "One of you is the messiah in disguise. But you are all ignorant of this." The master closed his eyes, and he was silent.

"The messiah?" thought the abbot. "The messiah is one of us? Who could it be? We are all so flawed; we are all so full of faults. Isn't the messiah supposed to be perfect?"

"But, then," thought the abbot, "perhaps his faults are part of his disguise. So which one of us could it be? Could it be Brother Cook? Brother Treasurer? Brother Bell Ringer? Brother Vegetable Grower? Which one? Which one?"

When the abbot returned to the monastery, he gathered all the monks together and told them what the wise master had said.

"One of us? The messiah? Impossible!"

But the master had spoken, and the master was never wrong.

"One of us? The messiah? Incredible! But it must be so. Which one? Which one could it be? That brother over there? That one? That one?"

Not knowing who among them was the messiah, all the monks began treating one another with new respect. "You never know," they thought, "he might be the one, or he might be the one, so I had better deal with each and every one of them kindly. I will speak gentle words. I will be considerate and helpful. I will give everyone the utmost honor. I will smile and be pleasant all the time."

It was not long before the monastery was filled with new-found joy. Soon new students came to learn, and people came from far and wide to be inspired by the chants of the kind, smiling monks.

And once again the monastery was filled with the spirit of love, the spirit of God.

Can we all be like the monks? Can we all make kindness, goodness, and decency our constant companions? Can we all make selflessness and altruism our guides and our goals? Can we all be like the good people who, in the aftermath of the fire, reached out in compassion and love? Can we all capture the postfire response of caring and sharing and make it the cadence of our every day?

If we can, then the human spirit will constantly reverberate at its finest, and our world will take a giant leap toward transformation and harmony.

The Community Grieves Too

We quickly learned that we and our family and our closest friends were not the only ones grieving over the loss of our house. Members of our community shared our loss and our grief, not just for us, but for themselves too. For in many ways, our home had been their home or, at the very least, their communal gathering place.

Our home was always filled with people—the members and friends of our prayer group who came to worship with us; Ellen's clients and colleagues who came to consult with her; our co-workers who used our house to meet their own clients; people who came to participate in our seminars and workshops; people who came to teach us, to learn with us, to eat with us, to talk with us; visitors from all over the country who used our house as their Southern California base; friends who sat in the backyard in quiet retreat; wisdom teachers and spiritual seekers of all faiths, light-workers and healers of all traditions. Just the week before the fire, more than eighty people were in the house to greet a visiting rabbi from New York. We learned Torah, sang, and danced until after midnight.

One of the men from our prayer group spoke for the others. "We all need a way to publicly mourn for the house, to

remember all the good times we've had here. We would like
to hold a gathering at the house-site, where we can express
our feelings and shed our tears—a kind of memorial service
where we can acknowledge our loss and say good-bye to the
house."

Though I had never before heard of a memorial service for a
house, Ellen and I agreed to let it take place, for I remembered
a lesson that I had learned early in my rabbinate.

When someone dies, the eulogizer at the funeral praises the
life and deeds of the deceased and usually focuses on the deceased's most intimate relationships—with spouse, parents,
children. Those dearest relatives are often comforted by the
words of the rabbi, priest, or minister, who acknowledges and
celebrates their role in the life of their loved one.

But there are always others who are mourning too, people
in the concentric circles of the deceased's life—nieces and
nephews, cousins, in-laws, lifelong friends, neighbors, co-
workers, casual acquaintances. I learned that the eulogizer
needs to speak of them too, in order to recognize and honor
the loss and the grief of everyone whose life was touched and
affected by the one who is gone.

Ellen and I are "public people," and our home was a "public" gathering place. We wanted to be sensitive and responsive
to the feelings of the "public" who felt attached to the house
and wanted a way to express their sense of loss.

The service was held on a lovely, sunny Sunday afternoon
three weeks after the fire. Though notice of the service was just
through "word of mouth," more than fifty people gathered at
the site. They brought flowers and fruits and grains, symbols of
rebirth and renewal. One man had hand-carved a bird from
balsa wood, which he had painted in bold, bright colors. The
carving was placed at what had been the entryway of the

house. The well-known symbolism was self-evident but very powerful: the phoenix will rise from the ashes.

The service began with the singing of ancient words in modern melody, "To everything there is a season, and a time to every purpose under the heavens" (Ecclesiastes 3:1). Prayers were recited, and readings and meditations were shared; there were spontaneous "testimonials" to Ellen and me, to the house itself, and to the times we had all shared there.

The most moving moment came when our friend Dr. Gary Hartman read a psalm that he had written especially for the occasion. He entitled it "In This House."

I share it with you here not as a tribute to us or our house, but because it is testimony to the power of prayer, to the way that words—heartfully written and spoken—can express sadness and sorrow and, then, help the mourning process move from grief to healing.

> In this house of love
>> we watched the yearly cycle move, the seasons of the year, the seasons of our celebrations.
>
> In this house of tastes
>> we shared food and drink for body and soul.
>
> In this house of life
>> we met our new Torah, wrapping our children, honoring our Minyan.
>
> In this house of joy
>> we danced and sang and laughed as a people touching God once again.
>
> In this house of searching
>> we honored learning and received God's words on Shavuos nights.

A house of wonder animals, howling for joy with their owners and guests, and also a canyon house sharing the neighborhood with the wilder animals, coyotes and snakes and birds in native brush.

A house overflowing with the stuff of life and Judaism and God, in material incarnations and in spiritual essence.

A concrete-slabbed Southern California house of stucco and plasterboard and wood, surrounding the house of spirit; one house charred, the other lives on.

Let us touch the hot pain of loss:

May God give us the skills to mix our tears with these ashes, to prepare the mortar from which we fashion a new foundation upon which a fresh form will stand.

Amen.

These words represent the path that we can all take when we are faced with loss and are in pain—the path of articulating our loss, acknowledging our grief, confronting our pain, and moving forward toward reconciliation and recovery.

When our hearts are broken or our spirit is sad, we can try writing our own prayer, our own soul-cry psalm. We will soon realize that the words are not coming from our "left brain," from the rational, intellectual place in our beings, but rather, from our "right brain," from the place of our feelings and emotions. Our conscious, thinking—self-censoring—brain may not even be aware of the emotive writing that is flowing from heart to hand.

On paper we will see all the jumbled sensations that are swirling within: pain and anger and overwhelming sadness; the sense of helplessness and hopelessness; the glimmer of faith and trust that we can "hang in there"; the vision of the road—hard and lonely though it may be—that will bring us to acceptance and healing.

Finding a Need

With the service at the house-site, our friends were helping to ease our burden and to lift our spirits.

Yet, as much as they all wanted to help, it is hard to know what to do for a friend who is in pain, who, in this case, has lost everything.

One man—a very kind, very wealthy man—called and said, "Rabbi, I want you to know that whatever is mine is yours. Just ask, and it is yours."

This was an incredibly sweet, incredibly generous offer. But shall I really ask him for something? What shall I ask? Shall I ask him to feed me dinner, buy me a suit, give me $100?

This unbelievably magnanimous gesture—sincerely given and sincerely meant—was just too general, too theoretical, to be very practical.

The offers that most helped us—and most touched us—were the ones that followed the advice of the writer E. W. Howe: "When a friend is in trouble, don't ask if there is anything you can do. Think up something appropriate and do it." This good counsel follows a modern dictum that many already heed, known by its initials, F.A.N.A.M.I.—Find a Need and Meet It.

Imagine how moved we were when we received these gifts.

The local Presbyterian minister—whom I had never met—heard that, in the fire, I had lost the pulpit robe that I was going to wear to officiate at my sister-in-law's wedding. He came to the house-site with his own robe, handed it to me, and said, "Here, this is yours for as long as you need it." It was a very precious—and very practical—gift.

A friend came to the site carrying a large wicker basket wrapped in colored cellophane. It looked like one of those gift fruit baskets. When we opened it, it contained pens and pencils, yellow writing pads, a ruler, a stapler, and a box of paper clips. Another friend brought Ellen a gift box with the kind of tape recorder that she uses to record her client sessions. These friends knew that we would soon have to get back to work, so they gave us a few of the "tools of our trade."

A woman who lives in San Diego, whom we do not see very often, grew up in the same Chicago neighborhood and went to the same high school as I. A few weeks after the fire, I received a package from her that contained a three-ring loose-leaf notebook. In the notebook was a complete photocopy of her high school yearbook. Her note said, "I know that I graduated two years before you, and that this is a copy of my yearbook rather than yours. But I thought that it would provide some memory of high school for you." The notebook was even purple, one of our high school colors.

In this incredibly thoughtful gesture, this woman gave me back a tiny bit of my history that had been destroyed in the fire.

When friends are in need, when friends are hurting, the best way we can help them, the best way we can serve them, is to F.A.N.A.M.I.—Find a Need and Meet It.

Sometimes, we will do very practical things for our friends who need us. We will bring them dinner, or clean their house, or watch their children for a few hours, or take care of their pets for a day, or go to the dry cleaners, the bank, the post office.

Sometimes, we will do things that only we can conceive—and that our friends cannot even possibly think about—that are extraordinarily special and that bring untold gladness. For weeks, for months, after the fire, I would not have felt the loss of my high school yearbooks, and I never would have dreamed of getting them back. But, oh, how sweet it is to have the photocopy that my creative and thoughtful friend gave me.

We will be doing our friends the biggest favor when we find their needs and meet them. We will be giving them the greatest blessings of friendship and love.

Behind the Closed Door

Ellen and I were showered with the blessings of love that came from our many relatives and friends. But at the end of every day, no matter how many friends had been with us, no matter how caring they had been, the door closed and we were left alone—just the two of us.

The most intimate of all of life's relationships—the marriage bond of husband and wife—is supposed to be the most supportive relationship of all. When I am sad and hurt, I should be able to turn to my wife for comfort and encouragement. When my wife is despondent and in pain, she should be able to count on me for understanding and support. And that is the way that it is supposed to work for us—and for you.

Most often, one of us at a time is in distress or pain, while the other is in a "better place," less affected by the event or emotion of the moment and more able to be of loving assistance. That is why it is a myth that marriage is a 50–50 proposition.

In reality, it is often 90–10. I am in need and you are there for me; later you will be in need and I will be there for you.

But what happens when both wife and husband experience the same trauma at the same time? What happens when both husband and wife are filled with pain and sorrow at the same time? What happens when both wife and husband are so emotionally shocked, so emotionally wounded, so emotionally depleted, that each can do little more than concentrate on his or her own emotional survival? What happens when both husband and wife have no energy left with which to help the other?

Under circumstances such as this, how can wife and husband be of any assistance, any support, any nurture, any sustenance to each other? Under circumstances such as this, how do marriages survive?

Statistics tell us, for example, that there is an unusually high rate of divorce between husbands and wives whose child has died. Consumed by grief, mourning in different ways, unable to help each other through the process, husbands and wives lash out at each other in frustration and break apart in anger, or they slowly drift apart, crestfallen and disconnected.

I tell you with the same honesty and candor that is in the rest of this book that, after the fire, it was not easy for Ellen and me.

Though we care for and about each other, though we love each other deeply, though we wanted to be as supportive of each other as possible, we quickly realized that our reactions to the fire and to the losses we sustained, and our sense of how best to carry on with our lives, were significantly different.

We discovered that we were grieving over different things—not just what had belonged to each of us individually, but whole categories of things.

I was in greatest pain for the one-of-a-kind historical losses—my sermons, my books with the margin notes, my well-broken-in baseball mitt, the autographed picture of my rebbe, my grandfather's pocket watch, the Bible saved from the Holocaust.

Though Ellen longed for those kind of historical items too, she was hurting most for the aesthetically beautiful things that made our home so lovely—a little cut-glass vase that reflected the morning sun, the art that had hung on the walls, the exquisite Tiffany stained-glass lamp shade, the view from the kitchen window into the flower garden.

It was neither "right" nor "wrong" to miss what we missed or long for what we longed for. It was just different—very different. So instead of collectively grieving over what we had lost, we were grieving separately. Instead of having deep empathy for the other's losses, we were each caught up with our own losses.

We also felt very differently about what we should do and how we should live in the aftermath of the fire. The insurance company informed us that the provisions of our policy called for renting us a house similar to our home in size and amenities and filling it with rental furniture and appliances so that we could get back to leading our lives with as little disruption as possible.

Ellen wanted to act immediately. She wanted to find a house with the same space as our house, move in, and—even in the chaos that surrounded us on the outside—give us some sense of settled normalcy. Soon, she wanted to resume seeing clients in her home office.

I wanted to move much more slowly. I did not want to try to replicate the conditions or the trappings of our pre-fire life, because, now, everything was different. I thought that it was foolish to rent a house with a large walk-in closet in the bedroom when we didn't have any clothes to hang there. I wanted to rent a small two-bedroom apartment, where we could recoup and regroup over a period of weeks or months. Ellen could temporarily see her clients in one of the many offices that she had been so generously offered. I wanted to mourn in a "little cocoon" and slowly emerge back into life as the healing and new growth came to my psyche and soul. I felt that when we had bought enough clothes to hang in a closet, or enough books to require a bookcase, then we could think about moving into a rental house that had the space and the amenities of our own home.

Again, it was neither "right" nor "wrong" to want one kind of housing arrangement or the other. It was just different—very different. Instead of having deep empathy for the other's feelings and needs, we were each caught up with our own feelings and needs.

Most of all, our need to understand and reconcile the fire was very different. We both knew that fires happen; we both were sure that God did not single us out for some terrible punishment. And we both sensed that there was some great, as yet unknown, reason and purpose for what we were going through.

Ellen was content to let the understanding unfold in its own good time, to let God and the universe enlighten us as they will. I wanted immediate answers. I wanted the fire to make sense *now.* I could not move forward until I was assuaged by knowing and understanding the greater design. I wanted to confront the universe and God, not in anger or rebuke, but to demand an explanation and a plan. As in the face of any death, any loss, when someone or something we love is ripped away from us and we are left totally bereft and discombobulated, I wanted as much information and as much understanding as I could possibly obtain to, in some way, help me regain control of a situation that felt completely out of control.

Ellen and I wanted to get to the same destination of understanding. But our timetables for getting there were very, very different. Again, there was nothing "right" or "wrong" about either timetable, but instead of having deep empathy for the other's emotions, passions, and needs, we were each caught up with our own emotions, passions, and needs.

So how did we reconcile our deep differences? How did we help each other in our sadness and our grief? How did we stay married through our tragedy?

We found ourselves doing a "cautious dance" around each other, constantly defining and redefining our relationship.

Sometimes we talked and listened to each other. At other times conversation was just too painful, so we called a "time-out" from communicating.

Sometimes we held each other very tightly all night. At other times physical closeness felt stifling, and we slept in different rooms.

Sometimes we were powerfully drawn together in a siegelike "us against the world" mentality, because no one but the two of us could understand what we were going through. At other times we considered separating for a while so that we could each heal in our own way, without imposing our needs on the other.

Fortunately, because Ellen and I are both professionally trained in crisis counseling, we had an intellectual awareness of what we were going through. Even when our emotions overtook us, even when we were most in distress or conflict, we had the luxury of being able to stand outside ourselves—even if just for a moment—and have a sliver of understanding of what we were experiencing and feeling.

Even more fortunately, a friend—sensing what we were feeling—reminded us of the story of Moshe Lieb, the late-eighteenth-century rabbi of the little Ukrainian town of Sasov, who taught, "From a peasant, I learned to love."

This poor peasant was sitting at an inn, eating and drinking with the other peasants. For a very long time, he was silent. Then he turned to one of the men sitting near him, and he asked, "Tell me, do you love me?"

The other peasant replied, "Of course. I love you very much."

Our peasant was silent again for a very, very long time. Then he again turned to his friend and asked, "What do I need?"

His friend said, "I am sorry. I do not know what you need."

Our peasant shook his head sadly and said, "You say that you love me, but you do not know what I need. If you really loved me, you would know."

Reb Moshe said, "I understood. To know the needs of another human being, to feel her joy and bear the burdens of his sorrow—that is true love."

Hearing this story we knew that, hard as it might be, in the name of the love that binds us, we had to rise above our own needs—even if just for a moment—and respond to the other's needs. So, when I lamented the loss of the baseball signed by Babe Ruth, Ellen did not say "Hey, it was only a baseball." And when Ellen yearned for the little glass hummingbird that stood on the windowsill, I did not say, "What difference does it make? It was only a five-dollar piece of glass."

Our marriage survived because Ellen and I were able to tap into the core foundation of friendship, love, and respect on which our marriage was originally based.

We learned that we were grieving very differently, and we learned to respect each other's grief and each other's losses. We learned that since neither of us was right or wrong in our needs, we each had to honor the other's needs, even when they conflicted with our own. We learned—more than we had ever known before—to respect each other's space and place and sense of being. We learned that we would heal in different ways and at different times.

We learned to be guided and inspired by the teaching of Joseph Campbell: "Marriage . . . is the sacrifice of ego to . . . unity."

In Gratitude

Whenever we think of the warmth and the caring and the love that friends and relatives bestowed on Ellen and me and our neighbors, we are humbled, and we are deeply, deeply grateful.

It was these kind, selfless, and incredibly generous people who lifted us up out of the ashes, who sustained us, and gave us hope.

For our cherished friends, and for everyone like them who brings comfort and solace in a time of need, and for you—who will be like them when those you know are in need—we offer this old prayer in modern form.

To friends and companions,
brothers and sisters of soul and heart,
to all who give and receive,
who share and who trust,
in this place and every place,
to them and to us,
Everlasting love!

We ask
for grace, lovingkindness, and mercy,
soul-satisfaction, contentment, and peace,
for them and for us,
now and forever.

Amen and Amen.

4

OF ME

More than twenty years ago, when I was sitting in the hospital watching my first wife die, I said to the doctor, "You know, I am living Kübler-Ross" (meaning the then recently published study *On Death and Dying,* by Dr. Elisabeth Kübler-Ross, which taught that the terminally ill—and by extension, those in mourning—go through five stages of grief).

The doctor looked at me for a long, long time, and then he said, "Rabbi, you know too much. Don't think. Just feel."

How right he was.

I, who had been trained in this highly rational, intellectual age to be a thinker and to celebrate the workings of the mind as the highest good, was suppressing and ignoring my emotions. Rather than really touching the feelings of my heart and my soul, I was protecting myself by seeking a logical, scientific—and emotionally safe—explanation for what I was experiencing.

Thinking and Feeling

In the hours immediately following the fire, I saw myself doing again what I had done the last time I had faced bitter tragedy—thinking instead of feeling.

When the governor came to inspect the damage, he came, as he does to any disaster site, as a concerned but detached observer. But for him, this time turned out to be different.

Governor Pete Wilson and I have known each other for more than twenty years, stretching back to the time when he was mayor of San Diego. Although our politics are very different, we have always maintained a warm friendship. When he saw me standing in the ashes of my home, all of a sudden, the fire took on a very real dimension. It had affected not just anonymous, nameless constituents, but an old friend. Out of the range of the radio and television microphones, the governor spoke with Ellen and me for a few minutes, expressing his sympathy, offering his encouragement and support.

As soon as he left, the members of the news media encircled us. "Why did the governor stop to talk to you? How do you know the governor?"

As he had, a number of local reporters soon recognized me, for in my more than two decades as a rabbi here in San Diego, and because of the books I have written, I have become rather well known. I have been interviewed by a number of the print journalists, and I have appeared on the radio and television shows of many of the electronic reporters. Some are acquaintances, and a few are friends.

I found myself in a rather awkward and uncomfortable position. I surely did not want to be the center of attention, and I certainly did not feel detached enough to be a "spokesman for tragedy." But many of these reporters had been good to me when I wanted to promote a program or a book, so I felt that I could not just turn them away. Much to my unhappiness and my embarrassment, I found myself doing a large number of media interviews.

Yet I did not give very real answers to the questions I was asked. Before the first microphone was turned on, I made a quick but firm conscious decision: I would not make a public display of my raw emotions and bitter pain. So I "turned off" my feelings, and I gave the most rational answers that I could. I did not—I would not let myself—go down to that deep place where the real truth of real hurt resides, for I would not expose my vulnerability and my grief to a voyeuristic audience that somehow thrives on other people's pain.

My answers must have been "good enough," for more and more reporters came asking for an interview. One even quoted to me from one of my own books, asking if, in the face of my own tragedy, I truly believed what I had written about suffering.

Ah. Here I was on safe ground. I could raise the discussion to the level of a dispassionate theological debate about the nature of good and evil. My highly intellectual responses left my fragile emotions untouched and seemingly protected.

Though my thoughtful answers seemed to have worked for the reporters, they did not work for me. Here I was, hurting and in pain, yet I responded only from my mind, while my aching heart remained silent. Even a week later, when our old friend Sandi Dolbee, the religion and ethics editor of the *San Diego Union Tribune,* interviewed us for an in-depth piece that she entitled "A Test of Faith," I carefully kept my emotions in check. Sandi wrote a very sensitive and powerful article; her words—*hers,* not mine—made me cry.

It was then that I knew that I had to feel instead of think for as long as it took my pain to play itself out. My feelings—not my intellect—my heart—not my head—would reign. There would be no false machismo; there would be no denying the truth. When someone asked, "How are you?" I would not casually say, "Fine, thanks."

"How are you?"

"I'm not doing too well today."

My candor may have embarrassed some or made others uncomfortable. But "the truth set me free." I did not pretend; I did not feign or fake my feelings. I grieved and mourned in full view.

The Sense of Irony

And I wondered—more than once, more than a thousand times—if life were not only making me unspeakably sad, but mocking me and taunting me as well.

Just like everyone who tries to transform a house into a home, over the years we lived there, Ellen and I had spent time and energy arranging furniture, and putting pictures on the walls, and choosing curtains, and planting a little garden.

Our little corner of the universe was finally feeling livable and comfortable.

So, without even discussing it with each other, without being very conscious of it ourselves, we had each begun to take care of some things for ourselves that we had neglected for a long time.

I had not bought a new sports jacket in more than five years. In the early fall, I found some jackets that I liked, and that were available in my hard-to-fit size. When the fire came, I had two brand-new sports jackets—that I would have worn for the next ten years—hanging in the closet, still waiting to be taken to the tailor to have the sleeves shortened.

For a long time, Ellen had been looking for a small, portable air conditioner to cool her office from the heat of the afternoon sun. Three weeks before the fire, she finally found it. Only a few of her clients were able to benefit from her newly comfortable office before the fire came.

For months, we had been discussing how to best cultivate the grass in the backyard. Just before the fire, we had gotten organic sea kelp, which was spread over the yard. A week later, the grass was a blackened wasteland.

In the ashes, we were keenly aware that tragedy plays no favorites and has no timetable. And we were struck by the irony and the wisdom of the old Yiddish expression *"Man tracht, und Got lacht,"* "Man plans, and God laughs."

The Sense of Unfairness

And standing in the ashes of my life, I felt an overwhelming sense of unfairness. Ellen and I are—at least we try to be— good and decent people. We have dedicated much of our lives to helping others, and to making our world a better place. Our home was always open as a gathering place and an extended home for our community.

We had—I thought—done nothing to deserve this violation of our home, this total disruption of our lives. We had done nothing to deserve the anguish and the pain that was visiting us.

In my sorrow—and in my indignation—I had no energy, no motivation, no desire to do the work or make the necessary decisions that faced me.

"Where will we live?"

"I don't care."

"What shall we tell the insurance company?"

"I don't know. You decide."

Or even more simply: "Where should we have dinner tonight?"

"It doesn't matter. I'm not hungry anyway."

I didn't have the strength to face the people who came to help or talk to the people who called with concern. It was just too hard to summon up the energy.

I was struck with the realization of just how fragile life is: how one random event can seem to ruin all that we have built and sustained over a lifetime, how one moment can upset the delicate balance on which our lives teeter.

It wasn't long before all seemed hopeless. "How am I ever going to go on? Why would I want to go on, anyway, with all my precious things gone? How will I ever replace them? I can't. They are irreplaceable. How will I ever live without them? Why would I want to go on in a world that is so capricious, so unfair, so unrelenting in its randomness?"

One night as dusk was settling into darkness, I sat on the scorched ground in what had been the backyard, staring at the ruins of my house. Playing in my head over and over again, I heard the theme from the television show *M*A*S*H:* "Suicide Is Painless." Maybe it would have been better, I thought, if I had just sat here and let the flames wash over me. Maybe I would be better off dead—not having to suffer this great pain; not having to contemplate a life with so much that I loved gone forever; not having to rebuild out of the ashes, all the while knowing that my life will never be the same.

If the fire did not destroy me—it couldn't; after all, I wasn't even here—then perhaps I can destroy myself: "suicide is painless." I'll be gone, and I won't have to face the emptiness, the sadness, the pain; I won't have to face all the confusion and the hassles and the uncertainty of trying to restore and rebuild my life.

Part of what I was feeling is a natural response to still being alive when so much that was precious to me was gone.

I asked myself, "After what has happened, how can I ever be happy again? How can I think of laughing or even of smiling? How can I ever use the few things that survived the fire? Wouldn't that be a betrayal of all the other things that were lost? How can I ever, ever say that I am 'fine' when this horrible thing has happened to me?"

When a loved one dies, the questions are even more compelling. "How can I eat, how can I go to a movie, how can I ever, ever enjoy myself again, when he is dead and will never eat again, when she is dead and will never go to a movie again, when they are dead and will never, ever enjoy themselves again?"

What I was experiencing was the fourth stage of Kübler-Ross's five stages of grief: depression.

Of course, I was in no position to objectively or critically analyze my responses to my grief—I was just feeling, not thinking. But, clearly, I was depressed—very depressed.

My depression was part of the process. I could not fully grieve, I could not expect to move through the grieving toward acceptance and recovery unless I went through the depression. It wasn't pleasant for me or for those around me, but it was a natural, necessary part of the process.

Depression

In my depression, I learned a lot about depression.

I learned that when any of us is faced with bitter loss, when we are in pain from the blows that life delivers, we will, most likely, go through a time of deep darkness.

We may try to protect our fragile feelings by intellectualizing the experience—by trying to understand and explain it rationally. But this self-ruse will work for only so long. We have to feel the raw pain, we have to touch the very depths of our agony and confront our worst demons, before we can begin to heal.

We might want to surround ourselves with people who will listen to us, for talking brings all the emotions to the surface and gives them full hearing. When we can talk about our sadness and talk through our pain, it can be therapeutic and cathartic.

Or we might not feel like talking to anyone for a while. We might not want to be sociable or even polite while we go deep inside ourselves to wrestle with our feelings. Being alone with our emotions for a period of time is perfectly fine and can be enormously helpful. The only caution is to not stretch out the "alone time" for too long, lest we isolate ourselves—and begin to detach ourselves—from the world. Hermitage in mourning can be good; becoming a hermit can be very harmful.

We may feel the sense of irony that Ellen and I felt about the house being destroyed just at the time that it had become most comfortable. We have all heard of this kind of terrible, ironic paradox, such as the young woman who was troubled all the way through school, who got in with a bad crowd and was doing drugs; just when she had beaten the addiction and was back in school getting good grades, her car went out of control on an icy road, and she was killed instantly. Or we have heard about the man who worked hard all his life. With the income from his pension and the money he had set aside, he and his wife were looking forward to his well-deserved retirement. Two weeks after his farewell party at work, he had a heart attack and dropped dead.

We may wonder how we can possibly go on after devastating loss. We may feel helpless and hopeless. We may feel suicidal—wanting to rid ourselves of the immense pain, wondering how we will ever go on so scarred or violated or ruined or alone, wanting to join our loved one in death.

These are all the "normal" expressions of depression. They are the feelings that we will experience in intense grief. Some of these feelings may be frightening—after all, emotionally healthy people rarely contemplate suicide. But thoughts are not actions; they are just thoughts. Just because we "feel like" jumping off a bridge does not mean that we should—or that we will.

Depression can be a profound and a life-altering disease. But in the context of grieving over a severe loss—when it is embraced and honored for its role—it is one of the normal stages of mourning on the way toward eventual acceptance and healing.

Making Short-Term Choices

I continually swirled through the first four of Kübler-Ross's stages of grief: denial, anger, bargaining, and depression—all at the same time.

That now makes sense to me, because I have learned that the most recent scholarship affirms that Kübler-Ross's stages of grief cannot be separated into rigidly defined time periods. They meld into one another and overlap.

But, ready or not, there were some short-term choices that Ellen and I had to make.

We needed a place to live. The insurance company rented us a house, and, in a day—it's absolutely amazing what having a good policy can do—filled it with rental furniture; rental appliances; rental pots, pans, dishes, and silverware; rental

blankets, pillows, linens, and towels; and even rental tele-
phones, televisions, and wastebaskets. It was very practical, but
it was very painful. I was torn between relieved gratitude and
deep anger and sorrow. This is not my house. This is not my
bed, my sheets, my fork. I don't want to live here. I want my
house back. Why do I have to live here? If it weren't for the
damn fire, I wouldn't be here at all.

I needed clothes. At a local discount store, I bought some
basics—underwear, socks, a sweatshirt. At a local department
store, I bought a couple of shirts and a tie. Then I called Lands'
End, the catalog company from which I buy many of my
clothes. In an hour, with the help of a "personal shopper" and a
credit card backed by the money that the insurance company
would provide, I ordered pants and shirts and sweaters. A few
days later, a large box arrived. As I unpacked it, I was torn between the same relieved gratitude and the deep anger and sorrow that I felt about the house. I was glad to have some clothes
again, but why should I have to spend money to buy clothes
that I once had? And, besides—even though they were from
the same company—these new ones weren't as good as the
ones I had lost. These were brand-new; mine were well broken
in. These were this season's colors; last season's colors were
much better. These were a poor substitute; the real thing was
gone forever. I don't want this stuff; I want my old stuff back.

I needed to replace the components of my computer system. But even though I bought matching parts, the keyboard,
monitor, mouse, and printer just weren't as good as the ones
that had burned up. They worked, but they didn't work as
well. The keyboard didn't have the right touch; the printer had
new features that I had to learn. My writing tools—the tools of
my everyday trade—were different, and I was angry and frustrated and sad.

Worst of all were the books I had to replace. It is no easy task contemplating restoring a library of more than 6,000 volumes. If I ever choose to do it—which, most likely, I will not—it is a job that will take the rest of my life. Some of my books, of course, were so precious, so rare, that they can never be replaced. But most of the ones I need for my everyday work, the 200 or 300 sacred texts and reference books, are available in bookstores or by mail order.

It may seem like a simple task to go buy a book, to open it, and to read from it. After all, a book is a book. No matter what copy or edition, the book has the same covers, the same pages, the same words. But replacing cherished books is a daunting, a near-impossible, task. For my books were not just pieces of printed paper; they were my companions and my friends; in some ways, my parents, and in some ways, my children. My books held my energy; they held the intimate relationship between their words and me. The books I had read and used for decades held my encounter with the text, my wrestling with the word, my struggle with understanding. No new Bible will ever be able to replace the Bible where I met God. No new prayer book will have the stain of wine that I spilled, or the dot of candle wax that I dripped, while chanting the prayer.

The new books that I bought—with their crisp, unsoiled, unwrinkled, unmarked pages—shouted out to me of what I had lost. They made me yearn and long for the books that were gone. The new books may serve the utilitarian purpose of having information on a page, but it will be a long, long time—if ever—before they evoke the energy, the spirit, of the words that were consumed by the flames.

I want my old books back, for they—much more than furniture, clothes, or computers—had a life of their own. I am angry that the fire took them, and I am sad that I will never touch them or read from them again.

Each One, Unique

When we are suffering and in pain, nothing that we can get, nothing that can be given to us, will ever be able to replace what we lost.

Each book of mine that was burned up was unique; every item that was consumed held a special energy.

Every person who lives and who dies is a unique, special human being. No reconstruction or transformation can ever replace our violated body or spirit; no other person can ever replace our cherished one who is gone.

That is why our well-intentioned attempts to comfort are often so botched—and so offensive. It does no good to say to a man whose wife has just died, "You won't be alone for long. There are so many women out there just waiting for a man like you." Nor does it do any good to say to a woman who has just suffered a miscarriage, "It's all right. Don't worry. You're still young. You'll have many more babies."

Everything and everyone that we cherish holds a singular place in our hearts and an uncommon place in the universe. When we lose a precious and distinctive being or presence, it creates a gap in our lives that will never be filled. And that is as it should be, for we honor the uniqueness of each human being, of each object in the universe, that holds the energy, the spirit, of God.

Yet, we know, too, that in the ebb and flow of the universe, the sun sets and the sun rises; the tides roll in and the tides recede; one thing goes and another comes; one life ends and another begins.

When I was about eighteen months old, my mother gave birth to a baby boy who lived for less than three months. The death of my little brother was a tragic and an incredibly sad time for my parents, and it created a family dynamic that still plays out five decades later. But I often wonder, What if he had been healthy and had lived? Our "nuclear family" of two children would have been in place; my parents most probably would not have had a third child. But because my brother had died, and because my parents thought that the "ideal" family consisted of two children, a few years later, my sister was born.

Did my sister take the place of my brother who had died? Of course not. He, even in his few weeks on this earth, was a unique individual with a unique soul. He could never be replaced. But, if he had lived, my sister, most likely, would never have been born. Her whole life, everything she has already accomplished and everything that is still to be, everything her own children—and their children and their children after them—have already accomplished and everything that is still to be, would never have happened.

Confronted by loss, we learn a painful but a very necessary lesson: nothing new, no one new, can possibly take the place of that which is gone. But something new, someone new, takes its *own* place, plays its *own* role, and the universe continues in its never-ending cycle.

Making Long-Term Choices

It was—and it continues to be—no easier with the long-term choices that Ellen and I have to make. For, as time passes and we have to make the decisions that will affect us for years to come, the stakes have gotten much higher.

For all these months, we have often looked at each other in despair and bewilderment—and with a touch of sardonic humor—and asked, "What is to become of us?"

Tragedy causes all of us—Ellen and me in this case, you at the time of your own trauma—to examine and reevaluate our whole lives.

First, we had to answer the practical questions.

Shall we settle with the insurance company and build a new house on our land?

On one hand, that made the most sense. The land is spacious; a few of the trees are coming back to life. We can design a house customized to our lifestyle; it will be functional and beautiful.

But do we really want to rebuild on that land?

We spoke to a man whose house had been destroyed in the Oakland Hills fire five years before. He said that he had been very excited by the prospect of designing a new home, and that he and his wife had built their dream house on their land. But six months after moving in, he sold the house as quickly as he could at a significant financial loss. He said that driving home each night, all he could see in his mind's eye were the flames coming up the hill. If that weren't traumatic enough, he said that he felt as if he were living "on the graveyard of my old life."

Ellen and I did not see the flames, but the canyon from where the fire came—even though it is turning green again—is still right across the street. And the man's words echo and resonate deeply within: do we really want to build a new home on top of the ashes of everything we once owned?

What are our alternatives?

We could sell the land—if anyone will buy it—and, with the money and the insurance settlement, buy a different piece of land and build there. Or we could simply buy a house somewhere.

But we cannot afford any of the land we have looked at, and the houses in our price range that we have seen so far do not meet our needs, let alone come close to matching the house we lost.

Perhaps we should just take the money and never own a house again. Why bother with the responsibility? We'll just rent for the rest of our lives. But then we get less money from the insurance company—what is called "appraised value" instead of "replacement value"—and we have to pay tax on the capital gain on the sale of the property, and we lose the mortgage interest deduction on our yearly income tax. So what might be emotionally satisfying would become a financial disaster.

We had to ask the same kind of questions about the other things that we had owned.

Do we try to replace what we lost? Do we try to replicate it?

Shall I buy the same kind of clothes that I had, or should my wardrobe have a "new look"? Do I need as many pairs of pants, as many sweaters as I had, or should I have fewer clothes that I wear more often? Should we buy as many cooking utensils and baking pans for the kitchen, or will we eat out more and cook and bake less? Shall we try to buy back the same pictures that we had hanging on the walls, or find different ones? Shall I try to get back all the books that I lost from my full reference library, or shall I get just the books that I use most often and go to libraries or the Internet for the reference materials I will need? Shall I start a collection of baseball cards all over again, or shall I consign that activity to the pleasant memories of my life before the fire?

Perhaps we should decide to "travel light," to not be owners of any more things than are functional and necessary to our everyday lives.

I remember a friend from college in the 1960s who, in the spirit of those times, decided not to be caught up with material possessions. He made a conscious decision to own no more than 200 objects, all of which could fit into his Volkswagen "Beetle." A pair of socks counted as two items; a knife, fork, and spoon were each separate items. His own rule was that if he acquired something new, he would give away something he already had—if he got a new shirt, he would give away a book—so that the total number of his possessions never exceeded 200. It was an innocent and an idealistic way to live, but it made his point to himself and to his friends: he would not be attached to or weighed down by things. (The last I heard, by the way, this young man, now solidly middle-aged, owns a house and all its accouterments in the suburbs but is still active in political causes, most notably, working to save the rain forests.)

In the immediate aftermath of the fire, Ellen and I together did not own 200 separate objects. We did not have to choose to "get rid" of anything. Perhaps we should be like this young man in his idealistic college days, living as simply as possible, not owning anything more than absolutely necessary, not getting caught up in the competitive consumer society or the false security of material possessions.

Whenever I find myself thinking this way, I wonder if I am becoming a socialist or a communist, but there is still enough of the youthful Thoreau in me to admire—if not emulate—life at Walden Pond.

Before the fire, I had thought that my life was fairly well settled and secure. Now it is nothing but questions, questions, and more questions.

Making Life Choices

Seeking answers to the practical questions we face leads us to deeper, more profound questions—the kind of questions we all ask ourselves, especially at a time of trauma and upheaval.

These are my questions. Ellen asks herself many of the same kinds of questions, and we ask them together too. But for simplicity's sake, I'll just share with you the questions I have been asking myself lately, knowing that my questions and answers affect Ellen, just as hers affect me. And that because we are deeply committed to each other, we know that, at some point, our answers must converge.

I am almost fifty years old. I no longer have a house. I am no longer "burdened" with material possessions. My children are grown and live in different cities, far away from here in San Diego where they were reared. I make most of my living by writing and speaking—which I can do from just about anywhere. I am not "tied down" by any major responsibilities, either to people or to place. At this point in my life, and under these circumstances, I am free—I have the incredible luxury and good fortune—to be able to go just about anywhere I want to go and to do just about anything I want to do.

So, in the words of the old prayer, I keep asking myself, "Who am I, and what is my life?"

What do I want to do with the remaining years of my life—fifteen, twenty, or twenty-five more productive, working years and, God willing, many more years of enriching retirement? And where and with whom do I want to spend these years of my life?

In the aftermath of the fire that took away all my material possessions and all the records of my history, am I moved to rebuild my "before the fire" life? Shall I continue rabbi-ing and teaching and writing in stronger, more meaningful ways?

Or shall I try something new and different, going off in entirely new directions, making dramatic changes in my life?

Shall I stay in San Diego, where I have aging parents and good friends and places to rabbi and to teach, and where I have professional contacts and long-term relationships, and where I love the weather? Or shall I go "back home" to Chicago, where—despite the less than idyllic weather—my deep roots call to me? Or shall I go to New York, the heart of the Jewish and the publishing worlds in which I live and work? Or shall I take this opportunity to really "go home," to make my spiritual homeland of Jerusalem my physical home as well?

Can I leave here?

What obligations do I have to my children, who, every once in a while, want to "come home" to visit? What responsibilities do I have to my parents as they grow older, as they come to the time in their lives when the roles slowly and subtly are reversed, and the children need to care for the parents just as the parents once cared for the children? What responsibilities do I have to the people who are part of my prayer group, who have worshiped with me for years, who count on me as their rabbi? What obligations do I have to colleagues and friends who have been so supportive in this time of our need? What responsibilities do I have to the community where I have served for more than twenty years?

What obligation and responsibility do I have to myself, and to my place on this earth? Am I still challenged to bring meaning and worth, satisfaction and happiness, to myself and my world?

Is there an ultimate purpose to my existence? Or, in the words of the Bible, is it all "Utter futility! . . . Utter futility!" (Ecclesiastes 1:2)?

Shall I give it all up, go off to Tahiti, earn just enough to get by, and spend the rest of my days sitting in the sun, drinking fruity cocktails, and staring at the endless expanse of blue, blue ocean?

Was the fire mere chance, or was there a message in it, a message that said, "Wake up. Wake up and take inventory of your soul, take stock of your life. Wake up. Ask the right questions, and find the right answers that will chart the rest of your days and years. Nothing happens by accident. The tragedy of the fire is not in the fire itself, but the real tragedy will come if the fire teaches you nothing: if you do not examine your life, if your heart and your soul are not moved, if you do not grow in wisdom and in spirit. Wake up. Wake up."

Decisions

So, what did we decide?

What did we decide about life-changing choices? What did we decide about staying or moving, about this way or that to earn a living, about rebuilding or buying, about how we will lead the rest of our lives?

So far, we have decided almost nothing.

And, as much of an equivocation as that may seem, as frustrated as we may feel, as unsettled as our lives still are, not deciding yet is exactly as it should be.

The first and foremost lesson that we learned—for us and for you—about making long-term decisions after experiencing trauma or tragedy is this: put off deciding for as long as possible.

It is virtually impossible to make well-informed, wise choices in the midst of shock and pain. We do not think clearly; our emotions often outweigh our good sense.

This is especially true for someone whose spouse has died after a long marriage. After decades of sharing the decision-making process, after using each other as a "sounding board" and depending on each other's good counsel, making life-altering choices right away is too massive a task to take on alone, or even with the help of well-meaning friends or adult children. "Should I sell the house and buy a condo? Should I move to Florida? Should I move in with the children? What should I do with the life insurance money? Should I take all the pension money now? Should I keep my money in the bank? buy stocks? bonds? treasury bills? Should I invest for safety or high yield? Should I just give it to my brother-in-law the stockbroker to invest for me?"

In the confusion and pain, in the emptiness and loneliness, that death brings—or in the aftermath of the trauma that comes with any violation of our body or our spirit—unless an immediate decision is absolutely necessary, I have learned that we should delay making these life-altering choices.

The longer we wait, the better our decisions will ultimately be, for while waiting, a number of good things happen: some of the questions answer themselves without need for active choice; time and perspective permit some other decisions to become obvious; the emotions produced by raw pain give way to more rational thinking; and new opportunities arise that offer new choices that were not there before.

Delaying the big decisions does not mean that we are not getting on with our lives. It simply means that we are waiting for the best time and the best ways to decide, so that the greatest and highest good can come from our choices.

A wise sage explained this when he was asked, "What is the highest act a person can perform?"

The master replied, "Sitting in thoughtful meditation."

"Wouldn't that lead to inaction?"

"It *is* inaction."

"Then, is action inferior to inaction?"

And the master quietly said, "Inaction gives life to action."

Going Through the Process

Waiting to decide life-changing issues also helps us recognize and accept the process that leads to our healing.

Grieving and mourning is a process that takes place step by step and will play itself out in its own good time.

I have not yet fully experienced this reality in the aftermath of the fire, because I am still in the midst of the initial grieving. But I can attest to the existence—and the power—of the process, for I went through it more than twenty years ago when my first wife died. And, through the years, I have witnessed hundreds of congregants travel the slow but certain journey from searing grief to healing and recovery.

The grief process cannot be hurried, and it cannot be controlled, for once we are in it—once the process has begun—it is as if we are being carried downstream on a raft. We may be able to steer once in a while, but almost always, the currents will take us where they will. Now and then, the water will be smooth and soothing; just as often, it will throw us against the rocks and hurtle us from shore to shore. If we fight against the process too strenuously, it will just take longer and longer and be more and more painful. But once we accept the process as a process and give in to its inevitable flow, it will take us where we have to go.

Modern psychology calls this process "grief work."

The ancient Jews created a paradigm for doing grief work by ritualizing the process. Their deep insight into human nature and their gentle enheartening of the human psyche led to a series of rites and observances that are as wise and as effective today as they were when they were first developed more than two millennia ago.

In the period of time between death and the funeral, the shock is so great and the grief so raw that no real mourning can take place. So the Jewish sages taught, "Do not comfort the bereaved while their dead are still [lying] before them" (Avot 4:23).

The mourning—and the healing—begins at the funeral service. The mourner tears a garment as a physical sign of spiritual grief. The sound of the tearing cloth is a vivid auditory symbol of the torn and stricken spirit. The sound of the dirt falling on the casket in the open grave is the heart-rending reality of the finality of death.

Immediately following the funeral, a seven-day period of intense mourning known as *shivah* (which means "seven") begins. Because sadness and grief are so great, the mourner is relieved of everyday concerns and obligations. Traditionally, during these seven days, the mourner does not leave home, so friends prepare food and bring it into the house. Worship services are held in the home so the mourner can recite the special prayers without having to go out to the synagogue (except on the Sabbath, when the rites of mourning are suspended, and the mourner goes to join the rest of the community at the synagogue worship service). Friends come into the house to express sympathy and to lovingly remember the deceased. It is customary for the mourner to sit on the floor or a low bench, symbolic of "being brought low" in grief.

This seven-day period is a time of intense but controlled grief. It shelters the mourner from everyday activities, such as the need to go outside the home to conduct business. It provides time to remember the deceased, and it surrounds the mourner with caring, loving friends. *Shivah* leads the mourner on the slow but steady return up from the depths of grief toward a level of sadness that permits a slow reentry into the world and the functioning of daily life. It is the first step toward acceptance and healing.

Following *shivah* is another period of less intense but serious mourning called *shloshim* (which means "thirty"). It takes place during the twenty-three days following the *shivah* and, together with the seven days of *shivah,* makes a total of thirty days of mourning. While the mourner leaves the house and returns to work, many other activities—such as attending celebrations or weddings and being in places where there is music or dancing—are prohibited. During *shloshim,* it is also prohibited to go to the cemetery to visit the grave of the deceased.

Shloshim is the next phase of the grieving process—the return to the everyday world, with some signs of mourning still visible and with activities inappropriate to mourning still prohibited. At the same time, *shloshim* limits mourning by not permitting visits to the grave, keeping the mourner from excessive expressions of grief.

Beginning at the funeral, continuing through *shivah* and *shloshim,* and for a full eleven months following the death, the mourner recites a doxology, a prayer of praise to God, at each and every worship service. Called *kaddish* (from the Hebrew word meaning "holy" or "sacred"), this prayer is recited as an expression of faith in God even in the midst of tragedy and grief. Reciting this prayer for eleven months, the mourner slowly but assuredly moves through the mourning process—from acknowledging the reality of death, through intense grief, through diminishing grief, toward acceptance and healing. The one-month break between the completion of the recitation of *kaddish* and the first anniversary of the death permits the mourner to "let go" of the outward signs of mourning and to return to a more normal existence.

Each year, on the anniversary of the death, *yahrzeit* (from the Yiddish meaning "a year's time") is commemorated. A candle is lit, symbolic of the soul and the spirit of the deceased, and the *kaddish* is recited during synagogue worship services. If possible, the grave is visited. The commemoration of the first *yahrzeit*—the first anniversary of the death—is a vital part of the mourning process. It signifies the "closure," the ending of the mourning period. Though the deceased will always be remembered and loved, the mourner can finish mourning and return to life. The *yahrzeit* symbolizes that the healing process can now be complete. Often, in connection with the first *yahrzeit*, the dedication of the gravestone takes place, marking the final resting place of the deceased. This is another vivid and dramatic ceremony to close the period of mourning.

These ancient Jewish mourning rituals were given the status of Jewish law, which meant that they were to be followed by the mourner as if they were injunctions from God. Thus, by observing the laws, the mourner was, at the same time, being led through the process of mourning, for the rituals were designed with the underlying purpose of guiding the mourner through the psychological process of grief work.

Other cultures and religions have their own mourning observances, complete with their own unique symbols and rites, fashioned with the same designed—if hidden—purpose. For every spiritual tradition uses familiar, comforting, ritualized behavior to help its people through the pain and grief of the traumas and tragedies of life toward acceptance and healing.

If rituals of mourning and grief work did not already exist, we would have to invent them now, for though modern psychology has taught us of the process, grief work is not an intellectual exercise; it must be done at a deep experiential level.

If you are part of a spiritual tradition that gives you rituals of grief work, take advantage of them—submit yourself to them—when life hurts you. If you are not part of a community that has formalized rituals, then when life hurts, ask your family and your friends to surround you in love and to invent for you some little formal rites and observances that will lead you through grief work.

Grief work is hard—after all, that's why it is called *work*—but it is a great gift to our psyche and our soul. When life hurts and we are in pain, grief work is the best way—it is the only way—toward acceptance and healing.

Ellen and I—separately and together—continue through the process; we continue to do the grief work. And we eagerly anticipate the healing and reconciliation that is to come.

Ways of Grieving

It used to be that the community held certain expectations for those in mourning. For example, when a man died, his wife was expected to put on "widow's weeds"—severe, stark black clothing—which she would wear for at least a year. If she were to dress in any other way, it would create a community scandal, complete with accusations that she was not being faithful to her husband, even though he was in his grave.

For the most part, these kinds of community standards no longer exist. There is no "right" way or "wrong" way to grieve. The grieving process will play itself out from beginning to end, because we cannot hurry what only time and distance and perspective will heal. Nor can we be obsessive and refuse to let mourning ever come to an end. But within the process, each person will grieve in his or her own way.

Here are some things about grieving that I learned and that I gladly share with you.

You do not have to feel guilty or disloyal to the trauma or the grief—or to the loved one who has died—when someone asks, "How are you?" and, on that day, you can truthfully answer, "Fine." Nor do you ever have to meet anyone's expectations by being "fine" when you are not. Just because you were "fine" yesterday does not mean that you will be "fine" today.

You never, never have to respond to the well-intended but terribly insensitive questions that mourners sometimes have to face: "What's wrong with you? It's been four months since Harry died. Why are you still crying all the time? Don't you think that you could at least go out to lunch with me today?" Don't be offended, because your friend—however awkwardly—is just trying to help. But don't be intimidated either. Just smile and say, "Thank you for your concern."

Do what you need to do.

Less than two weeks after the fire was Ellen's sister's wedding. For Ellen there was no question: this was her sister's wedding, and whatever the circumstances, she would be there. But I had a very hard time deciding whether to go. I felt as if I were still in mourning—that I was in that period that Jewish law calls *shloshim,* the thirty days after the funeral. Even though the fire cannot be compared to the death of a loved one, I still felt as if there had been a "death in the family." My home was gone; my possessions were gone. My dream of an uncomplicated, stable existence had died in the flames. I did not feel like singing and dancing and celebrating. And I felt that if we went, our trauma might cast a shadow on the festivities and our sorrow might diminish the joy of Norma and Michael's wedding.

In the end, I went to the wedding weekend. I excused myself from a few of the activities that I felt were inappropriate for me; I cautiously but gladly participated in the rest of the festivities. It was hard, very hard, to be in the midst of all that joyous celebration when, just below the fragile surface, my heart was breaking. But the sincere concern of family and friends was comforting, and the infectious spirit of love that filled the weekend confirmed the promise of a better tomorrow.

And do what you need to do to bring yourself comfort.

Your family and friends will wrap you in their sweetest and most compassionate care and give you their most tender comfort. But they cannot know exactly what you need, for in that old and well-known Native American image, they are not walking in your moccasins. It is never helpful for anyone to say, "I know just how you feel." For even though his father may have died too, or she may have been raped too, or he may have been fired from his job too, or her house may have burned down too, no one else is you; no one else is in your place; no one else can know how you feel.

You can accept the care and comfort that is given to you gratefully and graciously. But don't let that take the place of doing what you need to do for yourself.

Not long after the fire, Ellen and I went shopping—not for the necessities like toothpaste and underwear, but for replacements for some of what we had lost. Ellen loves music—it brings great, great joy to her soul. She felt the need to quickly replace some of the tapes and CDs that were burned up (the records, of course, were gone forever). We spent many hours in the stores finding the music she wanted most. Because she knows the music so well, we had to find not only the pieces she wanted, but the recordings with specific orchestras and particular conductors. When she came home and put the first CD on the (rented) stereo, and her music filled the (rented) house, I saw a calm and serenity on her face that I had not seen since the fire.

I love fountain pens. I love the smooth ink lines they put on paper and the way they can help express my mood. In the fire, I lost some very fine pens that I had been using for decades, pens whose nibs were so well-attuned to my writing style that they were almost an extension of my fingers. It will take years to break in new pens, but soon after the fire, I wanted fine fountain pens again. The ones that I bought still seem like poor cousins to their departed and much lamented "relatives," but having a good pen in my hand, feeling it glide over the paper, and watching the ink gently flow from the nib brought me a sense of order in the chaos, a sense of stability in the turmoil.

Did Ellen and I *need* the music and the pens? No. There were many things that we needed much more. But for a few hours' shopping, we got back some of our history, and we restored some sense of balance to our lives.

This does not mean that trauma and tragedy are an excuse for a spending spree. It does not mean that in our grief, we should rush out to buy the Mercedes or take the cruise around the world that we've always wanted. Rather, it means that there are certain people and places and objects that can bring comfort to each one of us. Instead of fulfilling the myth that we should "be strong" in our grief, we are best to recognize our pain and our sadness, and give ourselves the gifts that will bring us the most comfort and best help us heal.

And in your grief, you need to take time for yourself, to do what you need to do, when you need to do it, in order to bring yourself comfort and healing.

Here, however, there is a caution. When we are allergic to certain foods, foods that can do us physical harm, it is exactly those foods that our bodies crave the most. Similarly, when we are in emotional pain, we may crave the very activities that will add to our anguish rather than relieve it.

That is why some religious traditions and faith communities use ritual to help mourners structure their time and activities during the grieving process—for example, Judaism's prohibition against music and dancing during *shloshim,* the thirty-day period following the funeral. These parameters around social conduct are to assist the mourner in doing grief work.

But religious ritual is designed for the majority and is not always sensitive to individual needs and proclivities. And, in its ancient formulation, it does not always take into account evolving consciousness and spiritual growth.

So when you need to "take time off" from your grieving, do not be bound or intimidated by any societal strictures.

Two days after the fire, our next-door neighbor went to play golf. (He had ingeniously saved his golf clubs from the flames by throwing them into his swimming pool. They were damp, but they survived.) Most of us wondered how he could possibly go play a game while his house lay in ruins. But for him, it was a way to relieve stress and, for a few hours, take his mind off his pain. There was, he reported, an unexpected bonus. With his powerful swings, he hit that poor little golf ball unmercifully. His shots were not very accurate that day, but he had found a great way to pound out his anger and frustration.

A number of people who had survived the Oakland Hills fire reported that the only way they could cope with the enormity of the disaster was to take one day a week "off." In place of dealing with the clean-up, and the insurance claims, and the lost mail, and the contractors and the builders, and the total disruption of their lives, they took one day a week for themselves, to recoup and reenergize. Many said that on that day they would leave the community and go into San Francisco for dinner and a movie. The "day off" was a way to relieve the stress and the tension, to distract themselves from the harsh realities they were facing, and to have a tiny bit of distance and perspective to help them get in touch with their feelings.

In your time of grieving, you may want to go to a movie, or go bowling, or go to the theater, or go hiking, or go to a sporting event, or go to choir rehearsal, or go fishing, or take a short trip, or do any one of the many things that you like to do. Do not let anyone tell you that what you are doing is inappropriate or that it dishonors the trauma you have experienced or the memory of your loved one who has died. Whether your "time off" serves as a release for your distress, or as a distraction from your pain, or as a few moments when you have time to think and feel, it is a precious gift that you give to yourself, a respite that you need and deserve.

And in your grief, laugh.

That may sound like a complete contradiction, but laughter has two very positive effects on the grieving process. First, it has a physical benefit. Laughing releases certain endorphins from the brain that help our bodies feel a sense of happy well-being. When we laugh, we begin to feel better.

Laughter also is life-affirming. It leads us up from the depths of sadness and despair. Sometime during the first week or two after a great tragedy, particularly after the death of a loved one, the family and closest friends will probably spend a few hours spontaneously telling hilarious stories and anecdotes about the deceased. A few days after the fire, we told silly fire jokes, and roared in laughter about being homeless and possessionless. We were "on the floor" with that rolling belly laugh that comes from deep, deep inside.

As a rabbi, I've seen mourners do this time and time again, and I remember one night during *shivah* after my first wife died when my family and friends and I were shaking in laughter over the stories we were telling. Far from dishonoring memory, laughter enhances it; far from dishonoring the deceased, laughter is a tribute to the fullness of his or her life and the joy that it brought. And laughter plays an integral role on the journey from grief to healing, for as Lord Byron put it, "And if I laugh at any mortal thing, / 'Tis that I may not weep."

Finally, in your grief, it is imperative that you safeguard your physical health.

In our sorrow, we often neglect our own needs—we don't eat, because we "just aren't hungry"; we don't sleep, because we "keep tossing and turning all night"; we don't exercise, because "who has the strength?" We become physically weak and highly susceptible to both mild and severe physical illness.

It is no coincidence that more wives and husbands die in the year following the death of their spouse than in any other year. It is not just emotional heartbreak that leads to their decline and death, but the lack of attention to good physical care of themselves.

Those who go through the trauma of so-called natural disaster are also at higher risk of illness and death. For in flood, hurricane, tornado, earthquake, volcanic eruption, or fire, the earth is stirred up, and, in its movement, it releases infectious and potentially lethal toxins. Those poisons can enter our lungs and our bloodstreams and cause harmful physical disease and damage.

In times of loss, when we least feel like taking care of ourselves, we must take most care of ourselves.

So the instruction that we must constantly give to ourselves is simple but vital: Eat! Sleep! Exercise! Take vitamins! Go to the doctor if you are not feeling well! Take very good care of yourself!

If you ever feel self-centered or selfish taking care of yourself in your grief, if you ever forget how important it is to meet your own needs in your sorrow, remember the story of the sage who recalled when he was a young man. One day, he saw his father-in-law, a watchmaker, grow impatient with the watch he was trying to repair. The young man offered to try his hand at the repair, and it wasn't long before he saw that there was nothing lacking in the watch's mechanism; only a tiny hairspring was twisted. He deftly straightened the twisted part and put the watch back together. The timepiece began to keep perfect time again. The sage then taught: So it is with us. Sometimes it takes just a slight twist, a minor adjustment to the broken piece, and the heart will beat normally once more.

Tragedy Transforms

When tragedy strikes, when tragedy calls us to examine and reevaluate our lives, if we trust our feelings, they will not betray us. Without surrendering to any external judgments of "right" or "wrong," our feelings will guide us and lead us through the grief process to our own balance and healing.

For, ultimately, tragedy has the power to transform our lives.

On the other side of pain and grief, there is always new strength.

In tragedy, we can become stronger, wiser, more self-reliant, more self-directed. That is why it is said—and, oh, how the metaphor ironically applies in our case—that we "go through fire," and that we are "forged and formed by the heat."

On the other side of pain and grief, there is always new hope.

That is why the psalmist assures us that our mourning will be turned into dancing; that our sackcloth will be loosed and we will be clothed in joy (after Psalms 30:12).

On the other side of pain and grief, there is always new possibility.

For every door that tragedy closes, another door is unlocked, another door opens, another opportunity arises.

Or, as the playwright Tom Stoppard put it, "Every exit is an entry somewhere else."

Thus, in the image of the psalm (Psalm 23), when we "walk through the valley of the shadow, we need not fear," for there is new light and new energy waiting for us. We are promised "goodness and unconditional love all the days of our lives," and we are assured a safe "dwelling in God's presence forever and ever."

5

WHY?

When I was in college, I took a philosophy course on the nature of good and evil. All semester, we studied the writings of scores of philosophers, each of whom had a different definition of the notion of good and a different reason for the existence of evil.

To prepare for the final exam, we spent hours and hours memorizing all of the philosophers' intricate theories, comparing and contrasting them to one another and wondering if we could possibly synthesize their significantly differing ideas into one working concept. We were sure that the exam would be comprehensive, thorough, and very difficult.

Imagine our surprise when the professor handed out a single sheet of paper with only one question on it. And imagine our consternation when we read the question. The final exam in this complicated and complex subject was one word: "Why?"

I am sure that most everyone else's initial reaction was similar to mine: the professor must be kidding. But then I realized that the question really encompassed everything we had learned. So I wrote and wrote and wrote, explaining each philosopher's theory of *why* there is good and *why* there is evil. I offered my own opinion as to *why* one philosopher's ideas were better than another's and *why* understanding the nature of good and evil is so important both in historical context and in contemporary application.

Most of my classmates wrote their exams in much the same way, but when our tests were returned, we had all received grades ranging from B to F. There was only one student in the entire class who got an A on the exam. In response to the professor's one-word query, "Why?" she had written only two words: "Why not?"

Standing in the ashes of what had been my home, I remembered that old philosophy class and its precise and penetrating question. And—even though my belief system and my theology provide me with fitting answers—I still asked the question that almost all of us ask when faced with evil and suffering, Why?

Why did this happen?

Why did this happen to *me?*

How could God let this happen?

How could God do this to me?

What have I ever done to deserve this?

How can a loving God who is supposed to care about me and protect me let me suffer like this?

As these questions flitted through my consciousness, I began to wonder: were Ellen and I being punished for some real or imagined misdeeds?

In our spiritual work had we somehow invoked evil forces upon ourselves?

Was our work bringing us close to the secrets of the universe and becoming so revelatory that God was somehow stopping us?

Don't we—who have spent a lifetime serving God and others—deserve better than this from God? Is this our reward for a lifetime of service?

Is suffering the inescapable fate of those who serve God? After all, look at Noah, at Moses, at Aaron, at Jeremiah, at Jonah, at Jesus. They all served God, but they all suffered mightily in their service. Is this what was happening to Ellen and to me?

The Two Types of Evil

I began to think about some of the philosophical explanations for the existence of evil that I had studied in that long-ago college course.

I had been taught that, for all its complexity and its seeming unfathomability, there are really only two kinds of evil: evil caused by human beings who have free will, and random happenstance evil.

Much of the evil in our world comes from human beings purposely choosing to use their free will to do devastating evil instead of good. When a store clerk is beaten during a holdup, when a little child is sexually abused, when an innocent bystander is killed during a drive-by shooting, it is because a human being has chosen to do evil.

Even when suffering comes about because of "mechanical failure" rather than "human error"—when the airplane crashes or the car goes out of control—human beings are still responsible because, unwittingly, they manufactured a faulty product or they did not tighten the brake or the bolt well enough.

When evil and suffering are on a grand scale, the source is still most often the freewill choices made by human beings. Nations and governments do not crush the human spirit, or persecute or torture human beings, or make war. Presidents and generals—somebody's daddy or grandma—choose conflict instead of harmony, war instead of peace.

In our recent memory, the horrific evil of the Holocaust came from the darkly evil intent of one man, and the legions of ordinary people who readily joined him, using freewill choice to move a nation to the most unspeakable evil ever imagined. Other men and women eventually used their free will to overcome the madman, but the untold pain and suffering that was experienced by the innocent victims has given human evil a new and despicable face never before seen so clearly in human history.

The second kind of evil seems to defy any rational explanation. This evil seems to have its source not in any act or omission of any human being, not in the freewill choice to do good or evil, but in random, capricious happenstance.

This is the evil and suffering of children born damaged and defective, of debilitating, painful disease, of sudden, inexplicable death.

Sometimes we can find a logical explanation: the DNA was flawed or damaged; there was a genetic history of disease in the family. Yet just as often, there seems to be no reason for the evil and suffering—it just seems like an arbitrary, chance occurrence.

Discerning Evil

The fire that destroyed our house can be attributed to both these kinds of evil.

Though we still do not know the origin, it is quite possible that the fire was caused by evil done by a human being. Intentionally, someone may have committed arson, starting the fire in a freewill act of evil. Unintentionally, someone may have thrown a cigarette butt out of a car window, or left a campfire smoldering, or let a muffler dangle from a car, causing sparks to fly when the hot metal was dragged along the street.

Or the suffering that we have experienced may be because Ellen and I, using our free will, brought evil upon ourselves.

We knew that so-called natural disaster—a flood, a hurricane, a tornado, a volcanic eruption, a fire—is nothing more than a simple act of nature, of the earth playing out its natural order. This natural phenomenon is called a "natural disaster"—it is considered evil—only when it affects human beings.

If we and our neighbors had not had houses on that canyon edge, the fire that has caused us so much suffering would have been merely another forest fire, consuming acres of uninhabited land. But we all used our free will to choose to buy houses in a place where we knew that Southern California brushfires might come during hot, dry days with hot winds blowing.

We compounded our choice when we were given clear warning of potential danger but did not do anything about it.

About a year before this fire, there had been another fire in the canyon. It was a slow-moving fire that came about halfway through the canyon in three hours. (The fire that consumed our house came through the entire canyon in fifteen minutes.) The fire department had plenty of time and equipment to put out the fire before it caused damage to any homes. But, having experienced that earlier fire, and being aware of the possible consequences of another fire, we chose to do nothing.

We could have sold the house and moved away. We could have put a tile roof on the house, possibly protecting it from fire. (The only houses in our little neighborhood that survived the fire were the ones with tile roofs.) We could have found out who owns the canyon and demanded that the brush be cut back, removing a potential fuel source from advancing flames.

But we used our free will to do nothing—not because we wanted to bring evil and suffering upon ourselves—but because we were too complacent, too lazy, perhaps too arrogant, to act. In part, it was our inaction, our freewill choice, that brought us evil and suffering, and we have to take some responsibility for our choice and its consequences.

Now we better understand the words of the great sage Mahatma Gandhi, who said, "I have only three enemies. My favorite enemy, the one most easily influenced for the better, is the British Empire. My second enemy, the Indian people, is far more difficult. But my most formidable opponent is a man named Gandhi. With him I seem to have very little influence."

The fire was, of course, also the result of random, happenstance evil. Fires happen. Fires happen especially in Southern California where the brush is dry and the hot air whips up the flames. Our house just happened to be in the way of a fire that was burning out of control. That our house was destroyed was mere chance, a total fluke, a matter of dumb luck.

Dumb luck? Mere chance? Our entire life has been turned upside down by mere chance?

Facing the hard realities brought, in part, by this arbitrary capriciousness of random chance, I am tempted to ask now, more than ever before, "Why? Why my house? Why me?"

Explaining Evil

Throughout history, every philosophical system, every religion, every spiritual tradition, and almost every culture has tried to explain the existence of random evil.

Various philosophers have offered theories.

Some say that the world is made of contrasting opposites. Without night, we would not know day; without dark, we would not know light; without tart, we would not know sweet. And without evil, we would not know what is good. As the Chasidic rabbi Menachem Mendel of Kotzk put it, "A person cannot be consciously good unless he knows evil. No one can appreciate pleasure unless he has tasted bitterness."

Others disagree, saying that the existence of evil is a matter of the unconditional nature of God's completeness. A whole God contains all possibilities, so good and evil are two of the infinite possibilities of God. God's role is explained in the words of the prophet Isaiah, "I am God, there is nothing else. I form light and create darkness, I make peace and create evil. I, the Source and Substance of all do this" (Isaiah 45:6–7).

Some say that suffering is the way that we learn how to overcome the obstacles that are placed before us. That is why Rabbi Zusya of Hanipol prayed, "Thank you, God, for making me blind so that I might be able to see the inner light."

Others add that obstacles are given to us to make our desire, our ambition, our intentions, even stronger. The more we strive to find what is hidden from us, the greater the chance that we will find it. As the Bratzlaver Rebbe taught, "Do not be frustrated by the obstacles you encounter on your journey. They are there by design to increase your desire for the goal you seek."

Some say that obstacles are given, that we are confronted with evil and suffering, so that after surmounting the most difficult barriers we will be more fully worthy of coming into the presence of God. As Reb Nachman taught, "The battles against obstacles mold a person into a vessel ready to receive holiness."

Monotheistic religions posit that all the moral codes that define good are flawed, except one.

The most well known moral codes derive their authority from a variety of sources: from human reason (this kind of behavior makes rational sense), from human emotion (this kind of behavior makes me feel good), from human intuition (this kind of behavior seems right in my "gut," at the deepest core of my being), from societal norms (the consensus of our society agrees that this behavior is for the greatest good).

Though all these codes have many positive aspects in defining good and in determining good human behavior, they are all equally flawed. Human reason, human emotion, and human intuition can fail to think, to feel, or to sense the ultimate good, and we can be convinced of, be swayed to, or rationalize away the darkest evil. Societal norms can be distorted by evil people with evil purpose—Nazi Germany being the prime example. All these codes are subject to situation, circumstance, whim, or caprice.

The only moral code that is not affected by time or place— the only code with universal, eternal definition of right and wrong—is the moral code given by God. Called Ethical Monotheism, the basis of God's moral standards is that the authority is in the Author. Right is right and wrong is wrong *because God said so.*

There are two objections to Ethical Monotheism that keep it from being universally embraced.

Some believe that they have a direct and singular "pipeline" to God, which affirms their sense of God's will while rejecting all differing interpretations. Thus, throughout human history, much evil has been done *in the name of God* by those who claim that their will is God's will.

Others completely reject belief in God and, thus, a moral authority that is sourced in God. We can only begin to imagine the evil that human beings who recognize no authority higher than themselves are capable of committing.

Various religions and faith communities offer additional theories of their own.

Hinduism teaches that by meeting and overcoming evil in this lifetime a soul further evolves toward ultimate perfection.

Buddhism teaches that we must free ourselves of our narrow—unenlightened—conceptions of what reality is and what we want. In embracing the broadest view of life, we realize that our needs are only illusory. If we had no expectation of what others call good, we would not feel disappointment or pain in the face of what others call evil.

Christianity teaches that suffering has been revealed as redemptive—that there is ultimate meaning in suffering—for us and for the world around us because of the suffering of Jesus Christ. For those who profess belief in Jesus, there will be eternal reward, so any suffering we may experience in this lifetime is of little consequence in anticipation of eternity with God.

Islam teaches that evil and suffering is the will of God. Those who endure pain are doing so for the greater glory of Allah, who will provide reward in the world to come.

Judaism has no single response. Some Jews say that the existence of evil is God's will, and that, even though we do not understand it, we must accept it. Others say that it is prelude to heavenly reward. Still others say that it is *bashert,* preordained fate.

But, in the end, Judaism says that the real explanation is that there is no explanation. There is no rational way of knowing why random happenstance evil occurs.

Accepting Evil

With no complete answer to the question, Why? I am left with the same response given by that young woman on the college exam: Why not?

Why shouldn't my house burn down?

Why shouldn't evil befall me?

Why shouldn't I experience suffering and pain?

God never promised anyone—certainly not me—a life without pain or anguish.

Indeed, God affirms that evil is a co-equal aspect of Divine being. Remember the words of Isaiah: "I am God, there is nothing else. I form light and create darkness, I make peace and create evil. I, the Source and Substance of all do this" (Isaiah 45:6–7).

Evil and suffering are part of life.

No one is immune or exempt.

On the High Holidays, Jews recite a poignant prayer that reminds us of our fragility, of our mortality, of all the adversity we might face in the coming year. The prayer asks, "Who shall live and who shall die? Who shall pass away and who shall be born?"

And then the prayer gives a long list of the many ways that our lives may be taken from us. "Who by fire and who by flood, who by sword and who by wild beast, who by hunger and who by thirst, who by earthquake and who by plague . . . ?"

I have been reciting this prayer all my life, but it was not until my house burned down that I really came to understand it.

I always thought that the prayer was simply a litany of the various ways we might die. But, I now realize, it is also a litany of the terrible things that might befall us, the traumas and tragedies we might have to face in the year ahead. By reading the Hebrew more carefully, we see that "Who shall pass away?" really means, "Who shall have to pass (go) through these things?" And "Who shall be born?" means "Who shall be *reborn* in them?"

The prayer asks, in this coming year, "Who shall have to go through fire? Who shall have to go through flood, earthquake, hunger, illness . . . ?"

"Who by fire?"

This year, Ellen and Wayne.

The classic example of human suffering is the ordeal faced by the biblical character Job. As a test of faith, Job was subjected to the most devastating evils, to the most horrid anguish. But no matter what befell him, Job refused to denounce God, he refused to renounce his faith.

Even in his agony, Job was able to offer a most thoughtful insight. His question echoes across the centuries: "Shall we accept only good from God and not evil?" (Job 2:10).

A modern prayer, written by the esteemed and beloved Rabbi Morris Adler, asks the same question. Ironically, years after he wrote these words, Rabbi Adler—and those who loved him—experienced the suffering of Job. For, on his own synagogue pulpit during a Sabbath morning service, Rabbi Adler was shot to death by a crazed young congregant whom he had been counseling.

When he wrote this prayer, Rabbi Adler could not have known of his ultimate fate, yet his words attest to his ultimate faith. Like Job's, Rabbi Adler's words call to us from across the years and challenge us to accept the totality of God's universe, both the good and the evil that life gives us.

Shall we cry out in anger, O God,
Because Your gifts are but for a while?

Shall we forget the blessing of health,
The moment it gives way to illness and pain?

Shall we be ungrateful for the moments of laughter,
The seasons of joy, the days of gladness and festivity,
When a fate beyond our understanding takes from us
Friends and kin whom we have cherished, and leaves us
Bereft of shining presences that have lit our way
Through years of companionship and affection?

When tears cloud our eyes and darken our world,
And our hearts are heavy within us,
Shall we blot out from our minds the love
We have known and in which we have rejoiced?

Shall we grieve for a youth that is gone
Once our hair is gray and our shoulders bent,
And forget the days of vibrancy and power?

Shall we, in days of adversity, fail to recall
The hours of joy and glory You once granted?

Shall the time of darkness put out forever
The glow of the light in which we once walked?

With the philosophers, we have some limited understanding and some worthy speculation about why evil exists. With Isaiah and Job, we recognize that both good and evil are aspects of God, and that by acknowledging the existence of both good and evil, we accept the totality of God and the oneness of the universe.

Yet nagging—and painful—questions still persist.

Did God survey the universe one morning and say, "Ah, let's destroy Wayne and Ellen's house by fire today"?

Was God in the fire?

Did God sanction the fire?

Did God sit idly watching while my house burned down?

Where was God?

Where was God, who protects me, when my house was destroyed?

Where is God, who loves me, when my heart is broken?

6

WHERE IS GOD?

Standing in the ashes of my home, a journalist who knows my work well handed me a copy of one of my own books and asked me to read what I had written. The words were from *Living Judaism,* in a section called "An Essay on Good and Evil": "God is not in the problem; God is not in the challenge. God is not in the desolation; God is not in the destruction."

She asked, "Now that fire has destroyed your home, now that evil is not just the subject of a theoretical theological discussion but is very real for you, do you still believe what you wrote?"

I said, "Remember what else I wrote." I turned to the next page and read, "God is in the solution, in the consolation, in the rebirth. God is in the response, the restoration, and the growth."

I said, "Look around. God is in the hands and the hearts of the community of loving friends who have come to hug us, and to cry with us, and to comfort us; to help us sift through the ashes; to bring us food to eat and water to drink; to bring us copies of pictures that we lost, and little gifts to restore some sense of normalcy to our lives. God is in the love that surrounds us and envelops us."

With our lives both literally and figuratively in ashes, Ellen and I and our neighbors were the grateful and humble recipients of God's love flowing through the hands of a community of caring and loving friends, of God's children doing God's work on earth.

These selfless friends helping us dig through the ashes and bringing us comfort reminded me of the woman in a hospital gently cleaning the festering sores on the body of her friend.

An observer remarked, "I wouldn't do that for a million dollars."

Without pausing in her work, the woman replied, "Neither would I."

They also reminded me of the words of the modern injunction, based on the ancient teachings of the prophet Jeremiah, that challenges and inspires us all.

> As God is gracious and compassionate,
> you be gracious and compassionate.
>
> Help the needy bride, visit the sick;
> Comfort the mourners, attend to the dead.
>
> Share your bread with the hungry,
> Take the homeless into your home.
>
> Help those who have no help;
> Be eyes to the blind, feet to the lame.
>
> As God is gracious and compassionate,
> you be gracious and compassionate.

Where is God?

When we all strive to be like God—when we manifest God-like qualities of love and compassion—then God is every-where we are.

Alone with God

Yet, no matter how wonderfully caring the community, no matter how deeply loving the friends, eventually the door closes each night and I am left all alone.

It is then that utter despair overtakes me.

(Even months after the fire, I write here in the present tense because, though the initial total bewilderment and searing pain may be over, though they are diminished by time and per-spective, it is never "really over." The pain and the grief still bubble up to the surface at will, and at the most unexpected times, so the questions I ask—and the answers I seek—con-tinue and continue and continue.)

When I am at the lowest of the low, the deepest of the deep, figuratively—and sometimes literally—I cannot get up. I can-not imagine anything ever being all right again. I am unspeak-ably sad and deeply depressed. I feel forlorn, and forsaken, and completely alone in a cruel and unrelenting world. All seems utter futility. I wonder if there is any reason to go on and, if there is, how I can possibly do it.

I ask over and over again, "When bitter tragedy strikes—you and me—when life really, really hurts, where is God? Where is God when I need God most?"

Recalling a little story that has been told for many years helps answer my question. This story has become so popular that it has been printed on bookmarks, ceramic plates, and refrigerator magnets. It is most often attributed to an anonymous author, but it was really written by a woman named Margaret Fishback Powers. It is sometimes called "The Dream"; most often it is called "Footprints." It goes like this.

One night I dreamed a dream.
I was walking along the beach with my God. Across the sky flashed scenes from my life. For each scene I noticed two sets of footprints in the sand, one belonging to me and the other belonging to God.
When the last scene of my life flashed before me, I looked back at the footprints in the sand. For some of the scenes, there was only one set of footprints. I realized that this was at the lowest and saddest times of my life.
This really bothered me, so I questioned God.
"God, You told me that when I decided to follow You, You would walk with me all the way. But I have noticed that during the most troublesome times of my life, there is only one set of footprints in the sand. I don't understand why, when I needed You the most, You would leave me."
And God said, "My precious child, I love you and will never leave you. During your times of trial and suffering, when you see only one set of footprints, it was then that I carried you."

When I—when you—am in deepest need, when the pain is overwhelming, when all seems lost, when I cannot bear it any longer, when all my resources are gone and I cannot make it alone, it is then that God says, "I carry you."

God is like a loving parent. God loves us, and takes pride in us, and rejoices in our happiness, and hurts when we are in pain, and wants only the best for us.

Like a loving parent, God would like to protect us from all harm, give us what we want, and fulfill our heart's desire.

But, like a loving parent, God cannot shield us from all harm and hurt. God cannot solve all our problems or take away all our pain.

No matter how compassionate, how merciful, how loving God is, life will still have its trauma and tragedy, its pain and suffering.

But, like a loving parent, God does promise to never leave us alone, to always be our friend and our guide, to be with us in time of trouble, and to give us a full measure of Divine support, comfort, and love.

I need God. I need God to be with me. So in the words of the psalms, "From out of the depths I call out to God" (Psalms 118:5).

I say, "God, I cannot do this alone. I need Your help. I need some of Your strength, Your insight, Your wisdom, Your fortitude, Your counsel, Your guidance. I need a measure of Your understanding, Your caring, Your compassion. I need You to be my friend, I need Your love."

And, in the words of the psalms, "God answers me" (Psalms 118:5).

God is right beside me, right with me, right within me. God gives me a full measure of care and comfort, protection and support, grace and blessing, sustenance and love. God holds me tight and catches my tears. God touches me with goodness and whispers tender words of consolation and solace.

God gives me strength, and lifts me up out of the depths of despair.

In the words of the psalms, "God heals the broken-hearted, and binds up their wounds" (Psalms 147:3).

Alone I cannot do it.
With God, I can do anything.

Turning to God

A modern poem by Annie Johnson Flint uses the biblical image of the newly redeemed Hebrew slaves to teach us that turning to God in time of trouble will bring redemption and salvation.

Have you come to the Red Sea place in your life
Where, in spite of all you can do,
There is no way out, there is no way back,
There is no other way but through?

Then wait for God, with a trust serene,
'Til the night of your fear is gone;
God will send the winds, God will heap the floods,
God will say to your soul, "Go on!"

And God's hand shall lead you through, clear through,
Ere the watery walls roll down,
No wave can touch you, no foe can smite,
No mightiest sea can drown.

The tossing billows may rear their crests,
Their foam at your feet may break,
But over their bed you shall walk dry-shod
In the path that God shall make.

In the morning watch, 'neath the lifted cloud,
You shall see but God alone,
When God leads you forth from the place of the sea,
To a place that you have not yet known.

And your fears shall pass as your foes have passed
You shall no more be afraid;
You shall sing God's praise in a better place,
In a place that God's hand has made.

Talking to God

For many, it is hard to summon up God; for many, it is hard to talk to God.

Perhaps we have not talked to God in a long time.

Perhaps we do not know how to talk to God.

Perhaps we are embarrassed at the idea of talking to God.

Perhaps our rational, intellectual being rejects the possibility of talking to God.

Or even if we are in intimate relationship with God, even if God is our good friend and constant companion, perhaps in our distress and confusion, we may not be able to find the words; in our pain, we may not be able to articulate the words; in our anger, we may not be willing to say the words.

Where is God—how do we find God—when we need God most?

Actually, finding the words to say to God can be the easiest part.

At time of trauma, at time of tragedy, many of us instinctively call out to God saying, "Oh, God, help me." Or we simply cry out, "Oh, God." These words are not just an involuntary or meaningless exclamation conditioned by societal norms. They are a heart cry.

Or, if we have not called out spontaneously, then we can begin the conversation by simply saying, "Hello, God. It's me."

Or, we can take the advice of the Bratzlaver Rebbe, who taught that the psalmist of old advises us how to talk to God amid pain and anxiety. Commenting on the verse "To You I will bring a thank-offering, and I will invoke the name of God" (Psalms 116:17), the rebbe said, "It behooves us to thank God for the benefits which we have previously received. After we have done this, we will discover that we can talk to God about relief from present tribulations."

Or, we can simply begin with "the sounds of silence." In deep meditation, we can find God.

Whichever way we choose to talk to God, we come into God's presence. And the dialogue has begun.

And when we are with God, God always listens.

If we simply cannot find the words to come to God when life hurts, we can say these poignant words from a modern prayer by Rabbi Sidney Greenberg.

> Disease and misfortune come without warning.
> The wrath of nature can sweep us away.
> Trouble and tragedy are our common lot.
> Disappointment and heartbreak visit us all.
> The good for which we strive often eludes us.
> Confusion and uncertainty frequently torment us.
> We are frail and weak.
> We stand in need of Your mercy, O God.
> Have compassion upon us, Your handiwork.
> Watch over us and protect us.
> Keep us from yielding to bleak despair.
> Keep shining before us the gentle light of hope.

Listening to God

Now comes the hard part.

The real challenge in conversing with God is not connecting, not talking, but *listening*.

For God always responds.

So we have to listen.

We have to really, really hear.

We cannot let our egos, or our personalities, or our arrogance, or our self-assured certainties, or our personal proclivities, get in the way.

In the words of the contemporary Twelve Step programs, we have to "let go and let God."

We have to surrender.

We have to open our hearts.

We have to open to God's word and become clear channels, enabling God's light to flow through us.

In the image of Rabbi Abraham Joshua Heschel, rather than seeking to impose our will upon God's, we have to accept God's will—and God's infinite mercy—imposed upon us.

Then we will feel God's comfort and solace; we will get God's guidance and counsel; we will experience a full measure of God's love.

Where Is God?

Where is God when I need God most?

The biblical psalmist put it this way.

> When evil men try to destroy me,
> it is they, my enemies and my foes,
> who stumble and fall.
>
> If an army would besiege me,
> my heart would not fear.
>
> If war were waged against me,
> I would still be confident . . .
> Even if my father and mother forsook me.
>   (Psalms 27:2–3, 10)

An army besiege me? War waged against me? Who can think of anything more frightening? My father and mother forsake me? Who can imagine anything worse?

Yet even at these most unthinkable moments, even when everything seems lost, even when life hurts the most,

> God is the stronghold of my life.
> God is my light and my salvation.
> God *will* take care of me.
>   (Psalms 27:1b, 1a, 3)

I humbly and joyfully acknowledge God's intimate intercession in my life.

I deeply appreciate God's protection and support; I am profoundly grateful for God's guidance and love.

Yet the question still persists.

How can God who loves me permit this evil to befall me, this pain and suffering to engulf me?

7

SOUL JOURNEY

Where is God when life hurts?

As I struggle with this age-old question—suddenly made so immediate in my own life—I have been made keenly aware of the deep truth of the old wisdom-saying "When the student is ready, the teacher appears."

A number of months before the fire, one of this generation's truly holy men came to San Diego.

Rabbi Adin Steinsaltz of Jerusalem is a brilliant and insightful commentator on sacred text. Over the past three decades, he has translated more than thirty volumes of Talmud (the 1,500-year-old compendium of Jewish law and lore) from the original Aramaic into modern Hebrew, and he has added his own massive commentary. More recently, he has translated fifteen of the volumes into English, complete with the translation of the traditional commentators, source notes, footnotes, explanatory materials, and his own commentary. These books are sold in commercial bookstores throughout the country and are, literally, changing the face of Jewish scholarship and learning.

In addition, Steinsaltz is a theologian and philosopher who has written more than a dozen books delving into the foundations and meaning of belief. And he is a mystic, the author of books that offer deep spiritual interpretations of sacred text and serve as a guide to worthy and meaningful living.

When Rabbi Steinsaltz spoke to a standing-room-only audience in San Diego, my sense was that most were expecting to hear him expound on Talmud or speak about the mystical teachings of Judaism.

But instead, he took a section of the Bible—beginning with the thirty-seventh chapter of the book of Genesis, the well-known story of Joseph and his brothers—and taught that chapter, verse by verse, word by word. It was an awesome display of the rabbi's depth and breadth of knowledge, his incredible grasp of the text in its many layers of meaning.

Yet, many—including me—were bewildered. The word-by-word explication of a biblical text can be a very exacting study. It presupposes basic knowledge of the story, and its underlying assumption is that each verse, each word, holds deep meaning. Those of us who came expecting a dazzling lesson in Talmud or a burrowing into mysticism were somewhat disappointed by this close reading of the biblical text.

Yet I knew that there must be more to Rabbi Steinsaltz's choice than we understood at the time. So I wrote in my regular column in *The San Diego Jewish Times*, "Who are we to know?

"Who are we to know what lesson the great Rabbi Steinsaltz—and God—had in mind?

"Rabbi Steinsaltz did not accidentally choose to teach biblical text; nor did he by mere randomness choose this particular chapter from all the chapters of Bible. There was good reason for what he taught us. He must have been giving us a lesson that is still too deep for us to comprehend now, but we will, one day, understand."

Are There Any Coincidences?

That was months before the fire.

A month and a half after the fire, my prayer group met.

In coming together on a Sabbath morning for the first time after the fire, we simply chose a convenient date when one of our members' homes was available for the gathering.

In preparing for the prayer and meditation service, I, frankly, did not concentrate very much on that week's regular Torah portion. Instead, because the particular Sabbath coincided with the celebration of the festival of Chanukah, I focused on the special reading from the biblical Prophets that contains the words "Is this not the firebrand plucked from the fire?" (Zechariah 3:2). I thought that these words were the most appropriate—and most ironic—for my commentary and teaching.

But when I opened the Torah Scroll—on the very first Sabbath after the fire that we held our prayer-group gathering; a Sabbath that we had chosen simply for its availability and convenience—the weekly Torah portion was the thirty-seventh chapter of the book of Genesis, the very chapter that Rabbi Steinsaltz had taught in San Diego months before.

As I began a simple description of the events of the story, words began to flow.

I am still not quite sure where the words came from—for I had no conscious knowing of what I was going to say. But as I listened to myself, I realized that, rather than teaching, I was learning. After having studied and taught this biblical text for decades, for the first time in my life, I began to really understand it.

Weeks later, I made the connection. I realized that it was no accident that, months earlier, Rabbi Steinsaltz had chosen this story to teach, or that of all the Sabbaths we might have chosen to reconvene our prayer group after the fire, we had chosen this particular Sabbath.

For this biblical text had a profound lesson to teach me about where God is when life hurts.

You are probably familiar with the ancient story.

Joseph is the favorite son of Jacob.

To show his great love for this son, Jacob gives Joseph a beautiful garment, usually described as a "coat of many colors." Joseph's brothers are very jealous.

Joseph dreams dreams. Rather than keeping his dreams to himself, Joseph relates them to his brothers and flaunts their interpretation—that his father and his brothers will bow down to him. His brothers are angry, and their hatred of Joseph grows.

The brothers leave to tend the flock, but rather than using the time and space between them to reduce the tension, Jacob tells Joseph to go off in search of his brothers. Joseph cannot find his brothers in the fields, but he comes upon a stranger who points him in the right direction.

As they see him coming, the brothers plot against Joseph. Although they would like to kill him, they settle for stripping him of his beloved coat and throwing him in a pit.

Just then, a caravan passes by, and the brothers sell Joseph to the merchants, who take him to Egypt. There, he is sold to a fellow named Potiphar, the chief steward of Pharaoh.

Meanwhile, the brothers dip Joseph's coat in animal blood and take it to their father. Jacob assumes that Joseph has been killed by wild beasts, and he goes into deep mourning.

In Egypt, Joseph goes to work for Potiphar, who soon puts him in charge of all his household affairs. Before long, Potiphar's wife takes a liking to Joseph and tries to seduce him. Joseph refuses, but Potiphar's wife will not be spurned. She accuses Joseph of attempting to rape her, and he is thrown into prison.

In prison, Joseph meets two of Pharaoh's servants—the chief cupbearer and the chief baker. Each man has a dream, which Joseph interprets. The interpretations come true—the baker is killed by Pharaoh, but the cupbearer is restored to his old position.

Two years later, Pharaoh has a dream that he cannot interpret. The cupbearer remembers Joseph's skill at interpreting dreams. Joseph is called from jail, listens to Pharaoh's dreams, and tells him that the dreams mean that Egypt is soon to experience seven years of plenty, when there will be an abundance of crops. Those seven years will be followed by seven years when the crops fail, and famine will ravage the land.

Pharaoh appoints Joseph as second in command over all of Egypt, telling him to store up enough food during the seven years of plenty to last Egypt throughout the coming seven years of famine.

Joseph gathers so much grain that storehouses overflow. When the seven years of famine come, everyone in Egypt has enough to eat, and there is so much excess food that people from neighboring countries and clans come to buy.

The famine spreads all the way to Canaan, where Jacob and his sons live; Jacob sends his sons to Egypt to buy food.

When they arrive in Egypt, the sons must come before Joseph to make their request to purchase grain. The brothers do not recognize Joseph, but he knows who they are.

Joseph accuses them of being spies and sends them to jail. Three days later, he permits them to return to their country with food rations on two conditions. First, they must immediately come back to Egypt, bringing with them their youngest brother. (This brother, Benjamin, is Joseph's only full brother, because they share the same mother, Rachel.) And as security for their return, they must leave one of the brothers in Egypt.

Brother Simeon remains as hostage. When the brothers encamp that night, they find that all their money has been left in their grain sacks.

Back home, they report all that has happened to father Jacob. He is unwilling to send Benjamin back to Egypt, but the famine becomes so severe that he has no choice.

When the brothers appear before Joseph for the second time, he is overcome with emotion.

Joseph tells his steward to fill the brothers' sacks with grain and to send them off in the morning. But he also instructs that his own silver goblet and the money for the rations be put into Benjamin's sack.

Soon after the brothers leave, Joseph tells his steward to overtake them and accuse them of stealing. They deny the charge, but the steward searches the sacks and finds Joseph's cup in Benjamin's sack.

The brothers deny any wrongdoing and throw themselves on Joseph's mercy. He replies that they may all go, but that the youngest brother must remain to become his servant.

Brother Judah pleads for the family and begs Joseph to keep him as the slave and permit Benjamin to return to his father.

Seeing their contrition and their devotion to one another, Joseph can no longer contain himself and says to his brothers, "I am Joseph."

The brothers are astounded—and afraid. But Joseph quickly reassures them. He sends them back to Canaan to bring the whole family back to Egypt. When Jacob and Joseph see each other, the reunion is poignant and bittersweet.

Joseph instructs his family to tell Pharaoh that they are shepherds and would prefer to live in the countryside. Pharaoh is very pleased to accommodate the needs of Joseph's family, and they go to live in Goshen. There, they live out the famine, prosper, acquire holdings, and increase greatly.

Hundreds of years later, the new Pharaoh enslaves the Hebrews, the descendants of Jacob and his sons. Generations later, God calls upon Moses to lead the Hebrews out of bondage and to take them to Mount Sinai to receive the law. Forty years after the exodus, Joshua, the successor of Moses, leads the people into the land of Canaan—which they rename Israel—God's Promised Land.

The Big Picture

What a story!

It is a story filled with so many of the elements of the human condition: love, favoritism, jealousy, arrogance, hatred, betrayal, deceit, accusation, power, control, fear, revenge, reconciliation, reunion.

And it is also a story filled with great pain.

At so many points in the story, the central character of the moment must have suffered greatly.

Just think how Joseph must have felt when he was spurned and hated by his brothers, when he was thrown in the pit, when he was sold to the caravan, when he was accused of rape, when he was languishing in prison.

Just think how Jacob must have felt when he assumed that his beloved son had been eaten by wild animals.

Just think how the brothers must have felt when they were accused of being spies, when they were accused of stealing, when they had to contemplate returning to their father without their little brother Benjamin.

They were all in deep pain. They felt lost, forlorn, abandoned. They wondered how they could ever go on; they wondered if it were worth going on. In their pain, any one of them—all of them, at one time or another—may have cried out, "Why me? How can God do this to me? Where are You, God when I need You?"

And—given their place and perspective—their cries and their haunting questions would have been well founded.

They were asking the question then that we continue to ask now: "Where is God when life hurts?"

Living their story, Joseph and his family experienced the suffering and felt the pain of each incident.

They did not have the perspective that we do. They could not stand above the story and look down on it from a vantage point of thousands of years. They could not, as we can, see the "big picture," the gigantic canvas on which the whole story plays out from beginning to end. Intimately involved, they could only experience the word and the act of the moment.

But, if they had had the luxury of perspective that we have, then Joseph and his family would have known the whole story. And they would have known that each and every individual element of the story—including the pain and suffering that came with each of those elements—had to be there in order for the story to come out the way it must.

For Joseph and his family—whether or not they realized it—were all participants in a Divine mission.

Everything they experienced was part of God's plan.

What they experienced in the present was *pre-sent* by God.

If Jacob had not given Joseph the coat, the brothers' jealousy would not have been kindled. If Joseph had not told the brothers his dreams, their hatred would not have grown. If

Jacob had not told Joseph to follow his brothers out to the pasture, and if Joseph had not met the stranger who gave him directions, the encounter between Joseph and the brothers would not have taken place. If the caravan had not come by at that exact moment, Joseph would not have been sold into Egypt. If Joseph had responded to the advances of Potiphar's wife, he would not have been accused of rape and would not have been thrown in prison. If Joseph had not been in prison, he would not have met the baker and the cupbearer and interpreted their dreams. If the cupbearer had not been released from prison, Joseph would not have been called to interpret Pharaoh's dreams. If Joseph had not interpreted Pharaoh's dreams correctly, he would not have been appointed second in command in Egypt. If Joseph had not been second in command, there would have been no plan to store up food for the famine, and many of the inhabitants of Egypt would have died. If Joseph had not stored up enough grain, Jacob would not have sent his sons to Egypt to buy food. If the brothers had not gone to Egypt, they would not have had enough food to survive, and Jacob and his sons might well have died in the famine. If it were not for the famine, and for Joseph's role in saving his family, the descendants of Abraham, Isaac, and Jacob would not have come to live in Egypt.

If Jacob and his sons had not lived through the famine, then there would be no Jewish people.

If Jacob and his sons had somehow lived through the famine in Canaan instead of Egypt, then the Jewish people would not have become slaves in Egypt; they would not have been redeemed by God; they might not have gone to Sinai to receive God's law, and they might not have journeyed to the Promised Land of Israel.

No matter what the momentary pain or suffering of any one person, each piece of the puzzle had to fit into its exact place, at its exact time, in order for God's plan to play out exactly as it was ordained.

The Divine Presence; The Divine Plan

As I related the story on that Sabbath morning, I realized that I was being taught that the presence—and the reality—of a Divine plan was not just for Joseph and his brothers in long-ago times.

It is for all of us—all the time.

My mind flew to the remarkable words spoken by God to the prophet Jeremiah, which I had always found hard to understand. Now they made sense as God's way of revealing how part of the Divine process works:

> Before I created you in the womb, I selected you;
> Before you were born, I consecrated you;
> I appointed you a prophet.
> (Jeremiah 1:5)

Before the man Jeremiah came to earth, he was chosen by God. Before he was born into his earthly body, God gave him a special mission.

How is this possible?

In order to resonate with God's words to Jeremiah, I had to move from my limited human consciousness; I had to be willing to momentarily suspend my demand for the intellectual, rational, logical explanations of the mind.

I realized that I—we all—have to open our hearts to touch the hidden secrets of the universe; to see glimpses of eternal knowledge and glimmers of the all-knowing, infinite consciousness that God teaches and that only our souls know.

Soul Mission

With an open heart, I learned from the combined mystical teachings of Judaism, Christianity, and Islam and the spiritual teachings of the Eastern faiths.

Every human being is created from two distinct but inextricably intertwined parts. Our bodies are of the materials of the earth; they are limited and they are finite.

Our breath is the breath of God. As the Bible teaches, "God blew into his nostrils the breath of life [the spirit of God] and man became a living soul" (Genesis 2:7). Our souls—that which give us life—are a spark of the Divine. As the Bible puts it, "The light of God is the soul of human beings" (Proverbs 20:27). Our souls are infinite and eternal.

When God spoke to Jeremiah, God was reminding the finite earth-being of the God-source of his infinite soul and of the preordained Divine assignment that was given to him.

God was reminding Jeremiah—and us—that, just as it was for Joseph and his brothers, everything we experience in the present is *pre-sent.*

What is the Divine plan, the Divine blueprint for Jeremiah—and for us?

We cannot know for sure, but, in the words of the old prayer, we can surmise that the ultimate Divine plan is for God and humankind to work together "to perfect the world under the Kingdom of God."

Together, as partners, our job is to make this world a place of decency and dignity, of goodness and compassion, of harmony and peace and love for every living being.

Each one of us, each individual soul, is responsible for helping to fulfill that Divine vision.

According to mystical tradition, when God created the world, God created every soul that was ever to come into body on earth.

Each soul has everlasting and independent existence.

The eternal soul dwells in the heavenly realm and is endowed by God with ultimate and universal knowledge.

Every now and then, a soul makes an agreement—called a contract—to come into body on this earth, in order to fulfill a specific assignment or mission or to work out a particular life issue (what the Hindus call *karma*).

So, at any given time, some souls are in the heavenly realm, and some are in body.

An old Jewish legend teaches that once and only once in the history of the world did all the souls—those in body at the time, and those from the spirit world—come together here on earth. That was the theophoric moment at Mount Sinai when the commandments were given, when God's will was revealed for all time. Every soul that would ever live in body had to be there to receive God's word, for God's holy law applies to every being in the universe.

The individual mission that a soul is in body to perform is different for each soul. Yet all missions have one thing in common: the soul enters a body in order to serve God, in order to help God move forward the Divine plan, the Divine blueprint, that God has for this world.

A person's soul's contract may take a long time to fulfill. Sometimes, it is fulfilled in a few weeks, a few months, or a few years. That is why some earth life spans are long and why some are short.

The Chasidic Rabbi Israel, who lived to a great age, explained, "There are those righteous ones who—as soon as they have accomplished the task appointed for them on earth—are called to depart. And there are those righteous ones who—the moment they have accomplished the task appointed to them for their lives on earth—are given another task, and they live until that, too, is accomplished. That is the way it was with me."

When a soul's contract is fulfilled, the soul leaves the earth and "passes away" or "passes over"—or, as we commonly say, "dies"—back into the world of the spirit. The Bible puts it this way: "The dust returns to the earth that it was, but the spirit returns to God who gave it" (Ecclesiastes 12:7). But the veil between worlds—between what we call "life" and "death"—is so thin that the Chasidic rabbi Menachem Mendel of Kotzk taught, "Fear not death. It is just a matter of going from one room to the other."

In the spirit world, the soul rests and is cleansed of imperfections that may have attached during the earthbound journey. It incorporates the karmic lessons that were learned—according to some mystics, up to seven in each earth lifetime—and adds the earthly experience to soul memory. The soul reenergizes and prepares for its next mission.

The next mission may be another earth journey—in what Judaism calls *gilgool hanefesh,* the "rolling" or "transmigration of the soul," or what is commonly known as reincarnation. Or the soul may move on to other Divine tasks in the spirit world.

Joseph, Jeremiah, and Us

God was not speaking to Jeremiah alone.

On a soul level, each and every one of us is selected by God to be in service, to be a prophet—a messenger—of God.

Because the universe is a freewill universe, the soul can choose to accept or reject its mission and God's charge, and can accept or reject the place that the mission will be fulfilled.

If the soul accepts the mission, the soul "signs" the Divine contract, and if the assignment is on earth, then the soul comes into body.

Yet our human bodies are delimited by time and space, so, in body, we cannot and do not have eternal, universal knowledge; nor are we fully cognizant of our soul contract. We know that our general task is to serve God, but we do not have a complete memory of what our specific mission is or how it fits into the big picture, God's ultimate plan for the universe.

Every now and then, we may get a "hit," an intuitive, inherent sense of what our mission is. That is often what moves us to make certain choices, to go certain places, to form certain relationships.

That is what happened to Joseph and his brothers.

All along the way—whether or not they understood them at the time—almost all of the participants in the story had "hits" of the Divine plan—those occasional inner revelations that we all experience. That is why, at certain points, some of the participants seemed to sense the deeper meaning of the events.

Potiphar engaged Joseph because he sensed that "the Lord was with Joseph and he is a successful man" (Genesis 39:2).

After interpreting his dream to mean that famine would ravage Egypt, Joseph told Pharaoh that "the matter has been determined by God" (Genesis 41:32).

When the brothers were accused of being spies, Reuben immediately linked their misfortune with their past conduct, "Did not I tell you, 'Do no wrong to the boy'? . . . Now comes the reckoning for his blood" (Genesis 42:22).

The brothers saw the hand of God in their plight, "What is this that God has done to us?" (Genesis 42:28).

Most telling of all is Joseph's understanding of the meaning of and the all-encompassing reason for all the events: "It was to save life that God sent me ahead of you" (Genesis 45:5).

It is the same for us.

We, who are on special mission on soul level, may get occasional glimpses of the Divine plan, but when we are in the midst of the story, when we are participants moment to moment, we do not have the perspective to see the "big picture," the greater whole.

Standing in the ashes of my house, I could not see beyond the immediate destruction; I could not feel beyond my immediate pain. Through my tears, I could not possibly declare that what happened was, somehow, for a higher good. But I could sense that I did not know all there was to know; I could imagine that somewhere deep in mystery there was an explanation that was not yet mine to grasp.

I thought of the story of the little bird.

Every day, this delicate little bird found shelter in the withered branches of a dried-up old tree in the middle of a deserted plain.

One day, a whirlwind came and uprooted the tree.

The tiny bird was forced to fly hundreds of miles in search of shelter.

Finally, it came to a lush forest, full of fruit-laden trees.

I knew that, during our lifetime as finite human beings, we will all experience both what we call joy and satisfaction and what we call pain and suffering.

I slowly came to understand that when what we perceive as "evil" befalls us—when we suffer from the pain that comes our way, when life really, really hurts because the emotions are very real to our earth-body, human feelings—we may not know the reason, we may not know how the story will eventually play out; nor do we do know what the results will eventually be.

All we know—and we can take great comfort in knowing—is that our emotions are part of the playing out of our soul contract, part of a blueprint far greater than our finite minds can ever understand. Our experiences are a part of the ongoing process of God's unfolding Divine plan.

From Out of Tragedy

We often try to rationalize away our pain and suffering by saying that it is for a greater good.

Indeed, many, many times, much good comes out of our tragedy and our pain—good that may very well be part of the unfolding Divine plan.

In 1969, in Coventry, England, the Rev. Simon Stephens was called upon to counsel a bereaved couple whose child had died. Even with all his pastoral training and his years of experience, the Reverend Stephens realized that he could not truly empathize with the great agony of parents who have lost a child. So he introduced this couple to another couple whose child had also died, thinking that in their common experience and their common grief, they might be able to be understanding and supportive of one another.

That initial introduction led to the eventual establishment of an organization called Compassionate Friends, which now has more than 600 active chapters throughout the world. Compassionate Friends brings together bereaved parents whose children have died, for mutual understanding, support, and friendship.

In 1978, First Lady Betty Ford publicly admitted her addiction to prescription medications. Following successful treatment at the Long Beach Naval Center, she spearheaded the establishment of the Betty Ford Center in Rancho Mirage, California. Opened in 1982—caring for people from all walks of life, including the famous and the little known—this center now enjoys a worldwide reputation as an outstanding facility for the treatment of alcohol and drug addiction. From out of her own illness, addiction, and pain, Betty Ford has given courage and hope to tens of thousands who go to get sober at the Betty Ford Center.

In 1980, in sunny Southern California, Candy Lightner's thirteen-year-old daughter, Cari, was killed by a drunk driver. Candy's grief and anger led her to establish MADD—Mothers Against Drunk Driving. Through educational campaigns and lobbying efforts on both federal and state levels, MADD has influenced anti–drunk driving legislation and heightened public awareness about the perils of drunk driving. Because of the efforts of the members of hundreds of MADD chapters nationwide, the incidence of drunk driving—and especially teenage drunk driving—though still significant, has greatly decreased. Each year, thousands of lives are saved through the innovative programs and the dedicated efforts of MADD.

In 1981, in Hollywood, Florida, six-year-old Adam Walsh was abducted from a shopping mall near his home. His severed head was later found in a Vero Beach canal, but Adam's murderers were never captured. From out of his almost unbearable grief, Adam's father, John Walsh, vowed to search for criminals in unsolved crimes. His resolve led him to develop and host the popular television show *America's Most Wanted,* which has been responsible for the capture and prosecution of hundreds of dangerous criminals who otherwise might never have been found.

In 1986, the popular *Saturday Night Live* comedian Gilda Radner was diagnosed with ovarian cancer. Her treatments— including both traditional and alternative medicine therapies—could not halt the spread of her disease. She died in 1989. During her treatment, Gilda found great solace in the Wellness Community in Santa Monica, California, a support group for cancer patients. To honor Gilda's memory, and to give other cancer patients the kind of support that Gilda had found in the Wellness Community, her husband, actor Gene Wilder, established Gilda's Club. Opened in New York City in 1995, Gilda's Club is a gathering place providing emotional support, lectures, workshops, and social events for cancer patients and their family and friends. More Gilda's Clubs are planned in the near future for South Florida, Michigan, Illinois, Tennessee, Ohio, Vermont, and Washington. One day, there will be Gilda's Clubs throughout the country. From out of the pain and suffering of her death, Gilda Radner has brought comfort and hope to thousands.

In 1994 in Hamilton Township, New Jersey, seven-year-old Megan Kanka was kidnapped, raped, sodomized, and brutally murdered. Her battered body was found in a clump of bushes not far from her home. Arrested, tried, and convicted for the crime was Jesse Timmendequas, who had twice before been convicted of sex offenses against children. He lived right across the street from Megan and her family, and, playing the kind neighbor, he had lured Megan into his room to see his puppy. The outrage and grief following Megan's death galvanized not only her family and her community but communities and government officials across the country. Throughout America, local and state governments have now passed "Megan's Laws," requiring that communities be notified when known sex offenders move in. From the savage murder of one little girl has come laws that will help protect millions of innocent children from the sexual predators who roam the streets and neighborhoods of this country.

Seeking the Greater Good

There is only one problem with this earthly attempt to see the good that can come out of tragedy.

No matter how great the contribution—no matter how many drunks don't get behind the wheel; no matter how many criminals are brought to justice; no matter how many addicts become sober—no matter how much the common good is served or what benefits accrue to others, the one who suffered the pain will inevitably ask, "Was it worth the price I had to pay?"

Are the lives of thousands who do not drive drunk worth the life of the one little girl whose mother founded MADD?

We cannot possibly answer this question, for we have no possible way of balancing the gain against the sacrifice—this life for that one, this suffering for that good.

With our limited understanding, we can only believe that everything we experience is all part of our soul contract and part of the ultimate Divine plan and, therefore, eventually for the greatest good.

So, with the holy Rabbi Levi Yitzchak of Berditchev, we can ask God, "Show me what this—that which is happening at this very moment—means to me, what it demands of me, what you, Lord of the world, are telling me by it. Ah, it is not why I suffer that I wish to know, but only whether I suffer for Your sake."

The Grand Dilemma

With all that I had come to understand about evil and suffering, I was still left with a grand dilemma.

I unequivocally believe that this is a freewill universe, that God gives us the ability and the power to make our own decisions, our own choices. I am sure, for example, that we can use our free will to do either great evil or great good. We can use our free will to either passively accept what is given to us or to actively shape and forge our own destiny.

I have always believed in the response given by the wise sage to the woman who complained about her destiny: "It is you who make your destiny."

"But surely I am not responsible for being born a woman?"

"Being born a woman is not destiny. It is fate. How you accept your womanhood and what you make of it—that is destiny."

My question, then, is: if we came into our body with an already contracted soul mission, then where is our free will during our lifetime? Aren't we merely puppets on the stage of God's play, doing God's predetermined bidding, being manipulated and controlled by God's will?

Aren't we subject to what philosophy calls "determinism," the mere playing out of a predestined role?

I sense that the answer to this troubling question is found in what the story of Joseph and his brothers teaches.

We learn that what is predetermined is the intent, the objective—the ultimate destination. How we get there, how we make the journey along the way, is completely open to freewill choice.

The ancient sage put it this way: "Everything is foreseen, but free will is given" (Avot 3:19).

The sage was describing a scene that I often witnessed as a child. When I went to the Museum of Science and Industry in Chicago, I loved to see the gigantic model train layout. When I stood right at eye level with the trains, I could see only a few feet of track, and I could see the train only when it passed by.

But when I went up to the second floor of the museum and stood on the balcony overlooking the model trains, I could see the whole layout all at once. I saw the operator controlling the switches, and I knew that in his hand was the power to do anything he wished with the train. If he kept a steady hand, the train would stay on the track and keep going around and around. But if he turned the controls a little harder, the train would speed up, go faster and faster, and, eventually—usually on one of the sharp curves—fall off the track.

From my vantage point, "all was foreseen." I watched the operator control the switches, and I could see exactly what was going to happen. But "free will is given." The operator could choose to do whatever he wanted with the trains.

That is exactly what happens to us. On a soul level, the tracks of our lives are laid out. From a certain vantage point—God's—everything that can or will happen can be foreseen. But we are given free will. And we can use our free will to control the switches of our lives—to stay on the track or to derail—however we choose.

The Chofetz Chaim taught about the verse from Job, "You number my steps" (Job 14:16). "A decree is sent forth regarding the number of steps a person shall make during his lifetime. But it rests within his choice to determine whether his steps shall lead him to good deeds or direct him in the opposite path."

A master teacher offers us another image.

We are tied to a long, long rope that is tied to a tractor.

The tractor moves forward in a straight line to its ultimate destination—the place where our soul has contracted to go in this lifetime. Yet the long rope has a lot of slack.

We can choose to shorten up the rope and walk in a straight line right behind the tractor. Or we can let out the full length of the rope and move from side to side, far afield. We can dig a furrow over here and plant a seed over there. We can sit under a tree or climb it. We can pause at a creek for a drink of water; we can stop to wade in the creek for a while; we can swim or boat down it. We can dawdle or move forward; we can slow down or speed up. If we give the rope too much slack, we might get lost for a while; if we grasp it too tightly, we might get pulled along faster than we wish. If ever we wander too far away, the rope will pull us back to the path.

If we choose to resist the pull of the tractor, we may be bruised or battered, for we *will* be dragged along. If we resist often enough or hard enough, we may be beaten or broken. The pull of the tractor—the fulfillment of our soul contract—

may give us wide berth and myriad choices, but the tractor will always move inexorably forward. For one thing is certain: no matter where or how we journey, we *will* inevitably get to our destination.

The Chasidic Rabbi Pinchas often cited the words "A man's soul will teach him." And he explained, "There is no man who is not incessantly being taught by his soul."

One of his disciples asked, "If this is so, why don't people obey their souls?"

Rabbi Pinchas replied, "The soul teaches incessantly. But it never repeats."

Simply put, the soul contract that we made, that we came to earth to fulfill, defines the destination. The free will that we exercise determines how we will get there.

Of course, while we are in the midst of the journey, we may not know or remember—because it is a soul-level decision—what the ultimate destination is. We are like the characters in the Joseph story. We experience only the words and acts of the moment. We do not know what vital role each element of the unfolding story plays. We do not know how the story will conclude. We cannot know if what we perceive as the pain and suffering of the moment is a component of what will eventually be the greater good.

Because we do not know the whole story, we cannot know whether we are using our free will to support or hinder its unfolding, to hasten or impede the fulfillment of our soul contract.

We are like the man in the old tale who came home from the marketplace pale and trembling. He told the members of his family that while he was walking around the crowded market, he had come face to face with the Angel of Death.

The Angel raised his arms, but the man fled for his life. He told his family that he had decided to take his fastest horse and leave immediately for the town of Samarra. In that faraway place, he would be able to avoid the clutches of the Angel of Death.

After the man left home, his son went to the marketplace to find the Angel of Death and to inquire about the strange meeting that had taken place earlier in the day. The son found the Angel and asked, "When you saw my father, why did you raise your arms, but not take him?" The Angel of Death replied, "I raised my arms in wonder, because I was very surprised to see your father. I did not expect to meet him here today, for I have an appointment with him tonight in the city of Samarra."

Being with God

As we come to reconcile our concept of earthly free will with the existence of our transcendent soul contract, we still ask: even though we are on soul mission, even though we are here to participate in the fulfillment of the Divine plan, how does a loving, caring, protecting God let us suffer in this lifetime? Where is God when life—*this life*—hurts?

God would never abandon us.

God is always with us.

So the real question is: are we with God?

The feelings and emotions that we call disappointment and failure, pain and suffering are part of every life. They come from out of the external factors of situation and circumstance that we all experience.

But real trauma, existential pain and suffering, come only when there is internal disconnection and separation from God.

When we are cut off from God, the painful realities of earthly life begin to dominate over our transcendental soul agreements. When we lose our intimate connection to God, life can become almost too painful to bear.

But as long as we stay connected to God, as long as we remain in alignment with God, we will remain in accord with our soul mission and in harmony with the universe.

We are like the master who was banished from his country.

When his disciples asked if he ever felt nostalgia for his homeland, the sage said, "No."

"But," protested one of the disciples, "it is inhuman not to miss one's home."

The master replied, "You cease to be in exile when you realize that God is your home."

God is our home.

We may be baffled by God; we may be disappointed in God; we may be angry with God.

We may confront and challenge God; we may argue and wrangle with God; we may wrestle and struggle with God.

But, in the words of Holocaust survivor and author Elie Wiesel, "We cannot ignore God."

It is always our freewill choice: We can succumb to life's hurts and suffering and blame God. We can turn our backs on God. We can sever our connection with God.

Or we can turn around and find God right in front of us.

We can be like Joseph, who, despite the pain of the pit and the prison, knew that there was a plan and a purpose beyond what he could see. We can be like Joseph, who knew that as long as he stayed connected to God, no matter what happened to him on the outside, he would be all right on the inside.

That is why some people maintain their equanimity, their confidence, and their good spirit under the most dire of circumstances. They may be pained by external realities and out-side experiences, but their inner core is not affected, because they are at one with God. They are in the hand of God.

That is why martyrs and saints throughout history have gone to their often gruesome deaths with praise of God on their lips. That is why so many of the pious could march into the gas chambers singing, "With perfect faith, I believe." That is why so many people with the most dreadful diseases can face their deaths with calm acceptance. That is why some of our neighbors were able to respond to the loss of their homes and all their possessions with composure, serenity, and dignity.

Those whose souls are aligned with God are those who will prevail over any evil, over any suffering.

No matter how much life—*this life*—hurts, when we are with God, God is with us.

At-one-ment

How do we remain in alignment with God? How do we stay "on the track" of our soul contract?

Our choice is made on two separate but intertwined levels.

Here on earth, we make the moment-by-moment choice to stay at one with God.

Even when our faith is sorely tried and tested, even when the fire is burning in our faces, we can choose to consciously and deliberately follow the instruction of the biblical psalmist who said, "I place God before me always" (Psalms 16:8).

We can be face to face with God. When we place God be-tween us and the fire, what we see is God. When we place God between us and the disease, what we see is God. When we place God between us and the murderer, what we see is God.

When we choose to put God between us and our suffering, we affirm our at-one-ment with God, and we align ourselves with the higher purposes of God's Divine plan.

Our choice to remain connected to God is also made at a soul level.

Do you remember that High Holiday prayer that asks, "Who shall live and who shall die? Who shall pass through and who shall be reborn? Who by fire and who by flood?"

According to the poetic imagery of the prayer, God sits with the open Book of Judgment. We, God's children, pass before God, who reviews and judges all our deeds from the past year. Then God decides our fate for the coming year.

In the metaphor of the prayer, if we have enough good deeds, we are inscribed for life, but if our evil deeds outweigh the good, then, we are inscribed for death. In the oft-repeated refrain of the prayer, the process is affirmed. "On Rosh HaShanah [the Jewish New Year] it is inscribed, and on Yom Kippur [the Day of Atonement] it is sealed . . . who shall live and who shall die."

This prayer has always been perplexing and disturbing to me, for we all know good and righteous people who die, and we all know less than lovely people who live on year after year.

But this is really a soul-level prayer that means that once a year our soul reviews its soul contract and decides either to renew it or to revoke it.

The second part of the prayer explains how the renewal takes place when it says, "But repentance, prayer, and acts of lovingkindness will avert the severity of the decree."

In earth consciousness, the rabbis and sages have interpreted this to mean that if we live lives of piety and goodness, then when we come to die, our time on earth will be deemed to have been worthy and worthwhile.

But on a soul level, what the prayer really means is that, if we stay connected with God, if we stay in God's presence—if we stay at-one with God—then the pain and suffering that we may experience on the human level will be superseded by the joy and the glory of maintaining our soul contract and fulfilling our soul mission.

Then, we can experience the deep satisfaction and the inner peace that comes when we use our free will to align ourselves with our soul's path and purpose.

Then, we can understand and embrace the real meaning of the Hebrew words of the prayer as the annual soul-level renewal of our soul mission.

"Who shall *pass through* adversity? And who shall be *reborn* through fire?"

This year, Ellen and Wayne.

Soul Understanding

The fire that destroyed our house and all our possessions took Ellen and me on an unexpected journey toward soul understanding.

What we ultimately learned is not just the popular notion that God will never give us more than we can handle. By coming to understand an ancient biblical text, what we really learned is that whatever God gives us, whatever our soul contract demands, whatever our soul mission puts us through, whatever earth suffering we experience, has cosmic significance greater than we can ever imagine.

Even though we may not be aware of its meaning at the time, everything that happens to us, everything that we do, is all for the highest good—for ourselves, for our God, for our universe.

For we learned that no matter how great the earth mystery, we are in service to God.

Serve we must.

So serve we will.

8

AS WE THINK

No matter what our soul contracts, no matter what grand universal design we are part of on a soul level, the realities of our lifetime on this earth are still realities.

For Ellen and me, reality is that fire destroyed our home and everything in it. Every material thing we had and cherished is gone.

For you, reality is that you have been diagnosed with a dread disease; or you were paralyzed in an accident; or you are going through a painful divorce; or your body or your psyche has been battered and beaten; or your husband, your wife, your child, has died.

We are hurting and in pain.

Terrible things have happened to me and to you.

And, now, we have to decide how we will cope with them.

That's right.

We have to decide.

Despite our understanding of our soul contract and our soul mission, despite our understanding of our fate and our destiny, temporal earth reality is still our temporal earth reality.

But how we respond to reality is up to us.

And how we respond to reality is all in our minds.

As the Bible teaches, "As we think, so we are" (after Proverbs 23:7).

Within Us

Justice Oliver Wendell Holmes taught, "What lies behind and what lies before us are tiny matters compared to what lies in us."

What lies in us is the ability and the power to choose, to decide.

And, the Nobel laureate Elie Wiesel admonishes, "Despair is not an option."

There are those who have been held captive as prisoners of war in the dungeons and the torture chambers, or as political prisoners in the ghettos and the concentration camps, or as prisoners of conscience in the jails and the gulags.

All who survived the darkness, the isolation, the beatings, the systematic attempts at brainwashing had one thing in common.

They refused to succumb to despair.

They all agreed: the captors could imprison their bodies, but they could never imprison their minds.

Their minds—their thoughts—kept them free.

There is a woman who was taken to Auschwitz when she was a sixteen-year-old. Treated like an animal, she was forced to live in a filthy, overcrowded, almost airless barracks. She was given nothing more than scraps of bread and potato peelings to eat. The screams of the dying filled her ears; the stench of burning flesh filled her nostrils.

On the very day she knew that her mother was taken to the gas chambers to be murdered, she was forced to dress in fine clothes and dance a delicate ballet for the camp commander.

How did she—and thousands like her—survive?

Holocaust survivor, psychologist, and author Dr. Victor Frankl explains it this way: "Even in such terrible conditions of psychic and physical stress . . . man can preserve a vestige of spiritual freedom, of independence of mind. . . . Everything can be taken from a man but one last thing: the last of human freedom—*to choose one's attitude in a given set of circumstances, to choose one's own way.*"

The woman herself put it this way: "One day, in the midst of that hell, I decided that they might control my body, but they would not control my mind. Right then, I decided that I would not be a victim. I decided to be a survivor."

She would not be like another former inmate of the concentration camps, who was asked, "Have you forgiven the Nazis?"

"Never," he replied. "I will never forgive them. I will always be filled with contempt and hatred for them."

"Then," his friend gently told him, "they still have you in a concentration camp—in the prison of your own mind."

As we think, so we are.

Thinking

Sometimes, it is a matter of point of view—of how our minds see a particular event.

A crow once flew into the sky with a piece of meat in its beak. Twenty crows set out in pursuit of it and attacked it viciously.

The crow finally dropped the meat. The crow's pursuers left it alone and flew after the dropped morsel.

The crow said, "I've lost the meat. But I've gained this peaceful sky."

Or, as a Zen master whose house burned down just like mine did said, "When my house burned down, I got an unobstructed view of the moon at night."

Sometimes, it is a matter of using the mind to exercise sheer will.

No one who was alive at the time will ever forget how Jacqueline Kennedy behaved when the president was assassinated. Her husband had been shot right before her eyes; pieces of his brain and splotches of his blood splattered her clothing.

She could have been consumed by the horror; she could have howled and wailed in her grief.

But she used the power of her mind—the sheer will of her conscious being coupled with her deep faith—to decide to demonstrate grace and dignity. With her gentle strength, she led us in mourning and toward recovery. An entire nation that could have stumbled under the weight of its bewilderment and grief was sustained on the thin shoulders of this gallant young woman who chose not to yield to evil but to overcome and prevail.

Sometimes, it is a matter of using our minds to convince ourselves.

The old Yiddish expression tells us how: *Red zech ein,* "Talk yourself into it."

Always, always, it is a matter of choice.

As Zen wisdom puts it, "Be master of the mind rather than being mastered by the mind."

Always, always, it is a matter of remembering: as we think, so we are.

Choosing

No matter what horrors we face, no matter what evil befalls us, no matter how great the pain and suffering seem to be, it is our decision how to react to our circumstances.

What we choose is not dependent on external factors. What we choose is an internal process.

We can decide to be the eternal victim. Or we can choose to be the triumphant survivor.

We can choose to succumb to the darkness and shut ourselves off from connection with the Divine, or we can choose to remain connected with God and our soul's purpose, and let the light flow through us.

The Bible puts it this way: "See, I have set before you this day life and good, and death and evil . . . the blessing and the curse. . . . Choose life!" (Deuteronomy 30:15, 19).

According to this biblical passage, evil is equated with curse and death; good is equated with blessing and life.

The admonition is: Choose blessing; choose good; choose life.

The choice is ours—mine and yours.

Overcoming

Sometimes life seems to bring nothing but pain and suffering.

But pain and suffering are defined by how we choose to define them.

And pain and suffering are defeated by how we choose to overcome them.

This poem, by an anonymous author, may help us remember how our minds make the choice. It is entitled—and addressed—"To Life."

Life, you have beaten me.
Still, with stinging wounds,
I kiss your hands.

Though you have tortured me
until my joy was crushed;
though I have trembled at your power,
and wept in terror, hour after hour;
For all our struggles and our strife,
I love you, life.

Though what I build, you will destroy;
Though what I seek and cherish, you will take,
Though you have snatched hope and will from my weak
    hands,
And though you break my heart and dispel my dreams,
I love you, life.

And life, for all your cruel powers,
for all your proud brutality,
How wonderful the brief few hours
when you were kind to me.

Forging Our Future

We can use our powers of choice to choose how to shape and forge our future.

This modern prayer by Rabbi Sidney Greenberg vividly reminds us of the choices we can make.

We look to the future with hope—yet with trembling,
Knowing that uncertainties accompany the days ahead.

Help us, O God, to look forward with faith,
And to learn from whatever the future may bring.

If we must face disappointment,
Help us to learn patience.

If we must face sorrow,
Help us to learn sympathy.

If we must face pain,
Help us to learn strength.

If we must face danger,
Help us to learn courage.

If we must face failure,
Help us to learn endurance.

If we achieve success,
Help us to learn gratitude.

If we attain prosperity,
Help us to learn generosity.

If we win praise,
Help us to learn humility.

If we are blessed with joy,
Help us to learn sharing.

If we are blessed with health,
Help us to learn caring.

Whatever the days and years may bring,
May we confront them honorably and faithfully;

May we know the serenity which comes to those
Who find their hope and their strength in You.

Giving Thanks

We also have the power to decide that we will come to God not only in pain, not only in anger for the curses we perceive are ours, but also in gratitude and thanksgiving for the many gifts and blessings that we have been given.

Once again, Rabbi Greenberg gives us poignant words to speak to God.

O God, to whom we come so often with needs to be satisfied, we come to You now in gratitude for what we already have and are.

For gifts beyond deserving or counting, we give thanks.

You have given us the ability to become more than we have been, the urge to be more than we are, and a gnawing hunger to attain heights only dimly imagined.

For the power to grow, we give thanks.

You have endowed us with the capacity to discern the difference between right and wrong; and You have enabled us to follow the right, to avoid the wrong.

For the power to choose, we give thanks.

You have blessed us with the ability to fashion things of beauty, to sing new songs, to spin new tales, to add to the treasure-house of human civilization.

For the power to create, we give thanks.

You have equipped us with the yearning to commune with You,
to bring You our fears and our dreams, our hurts and our joys,
our guilt and our gratitude; to share hopes and concerns with
You and with others.

> For the power to pray, we give thanks.

You have ennobled us with the strength to abandon our
transgressions, to overcome our faults, to mend our ways,
and to answer the summons "to turn to You with all our heart
and soul."

> For the power to repent, we give thanks.

You have fortified us with the ability to rise above
disappointment and failure, to go on after we have been bruised
and bereaved, to refuse to admit defeat and despair.

> For the power to hope, we give thanks.

You have enlarged us with the ability to cherish others, to make
their lives as dear to us as our own, to share their hopes, to feel
their hurts, to know their hearts.

> For the power to love, we give thanks.

We praise You and we thank You, O Lord our God,
For all the many blessings You have bestowed upon us.

> We praise You and we thank You, O Lord our God,
> For Your lovingkindness endures forever.

Reaching Deep

The power of the mind, the power of our ability to choose, is most dramatically illustrated in this story, which I heard from my colleagues Rabbis Jack Riemer and Bernard King.

It is a story about the world-renowned violinist Itzhak Perlman.

Everybody knows that childhood polio left Perlman able to walk only with the aid of two crutches and with braces on both of his legs. When he plays a concert, the journey from the wings to center stage is slow and laborious. Yet, once he begins playing, his incredible talent transcends any thought of physical challenge.

One evening, Perlman was scheduled to play a most difficult violin concerto at one of the world's most famous recital halls. He slowly made his way onstage, set aside his crutches, unloosed his leg braces, took up his violin, and nodded to the conductor to begin.

Only a few bars into the concerto, one of the strings on Perlman's violin broke, with a riflelike popping noise that filled the entire auditorium. The orchestra immediately stopped playing, and the audience held its collective breath. Most assumed that Perlman would have to put on his braces, take up his crutches, and slowly walk offstage to get a new string. Or, perhaps, an assistant would come out with a new string or a substitute violin.

But, after just a moment's pause, Perlman set his violin under his chin, and signaled to the conductor to begin again.

An eyewitness recounted, "Now, I know that it is impossible to play a violin concerto with just three strings. I know that, and you know that, but that night, Itzhak Perlman refused to know that. You could see him modulating, changing, and recomposing in his head. At one point, it sounded as if he were retuning the strings to get new sounds from them that they had never made before.

"When he finished, there was an awesome silence in the room. And then people rose and cheered. . . . We were all on our feet, screaming and cheering. . . . He smiled, wiped his brow, raised his bow to quiet us . . . and then he said . . . not boastfully, but in a quiet, pensive tone, 'You know, sometimes it is the artist's task to find out how much music you can still make with what you have left.'"

Letting Go

A well-known tale teaches us that in our minds—and in our hearts and our spirits—is the ability to let go of our hurts and our pain, to release ourselves from our suffering, and to put ourselves back into God's hands.

Two monks journeying back to their monastery found an exceedingly beautiful woman standing helplessly at the edge of a fast-flowing river.

Without a word, the older monk picked her up, put her on his back, and carried her across the water. On the other side, he gently set her down. She smiled at him, bowed deeply, and continued on her way.

The monks, too, continued on their journey, but the younger monk could not contain himself. For the next two hours, he berated his fellow.

"Have you forgotten our rules? How dare you touch a woman? How could you lift her and carry her across the river? Such behavior is entirely unsuitable for a monk. You have put us all into disrepute. What if someone had seen you? What would people say?"

The older monk listened patiently to the never-ending rebuke. As they neared the monastery, he finally broke his silence. He said to his companion, "Brother, I left that woman back at the riverbank. Why are you still carrying her?"

How can we put down our grief and set aside our pain? How can we bring joy back into our lives?

Everything we need for healing and transformation is within us.

And everything within us is sourced by God.

That is why the Bible teaches, "If you let God be your everlasting light, then the days of your mourning *shall* come to an end" (Isaiah 60:20).

Life happens.

Sometimes it will seem joyful and sweet.

Sometimes it will seem bitter and painful.

Like Itzhak Perlman—in the face of challenge, in the wake of tragedy, in the midst of pain and suffering—it is our task, mine and yours, to dig deep inside, to find life's perfection, to align with our soul path, to prevail over the obstacles, and to make beautiful music with what we have left.

As we think, so we are.

9

GROWING

Rabbi Alvin Fine reminds us of what we all know:

> Birth is a beginning
> And death a destination
> But life is a journey
> A going—a growing . . .

When pain and suffering befall us—when the fires of life burn us and threaten to consume us—it is our soul's way, and it is God's way, of waking us up to our expanded and ever-expanding purpose. It is an invitation to grow into our larger selves, to move up to life's next level of being and becoming.

Knowing Beyond Knowing

The wise crone grew old and infirm.

Her disciples begged her not to die. She said, "If I do not die now, how will you ever see?"

They asked, "What is it that we fail to see when you are here with us?"

The crone was silent; she would not answer their question.

When the moment of her death was near, her disciples said to her, "What is it that we will see when you are gone?"

With a twinkle in her eye, the crone said, "All I did was sit here on the riverbank handing out river water. After I am gone, I trust that you will notice the river."

We wonder.

Have we learned and grown enough, have our beings expanded enough, that we—with our finite, limited knowledge—can ever know God's ultimate plan for the universe?

The rabbi-author Chaim Potok articulates the question for us by commenting on a verse from the biblical book of Genesis. "And God saw all that He had made, and behold it was good" (Genesis 1:31).

Potok says, "The seeing of God is not like the seeing of man. Man sees only between the blinks of his eyes. He does not know what the world is like during the blinks. He sees the world in pieces, in fragments. But God sees the world whole, unbroken. That world is good. Our seeing is broken. Can we make it like the world of God?"

The late mystic Rabbi Abraham Joshua Heschel answers Potok by suggesting that every once in a while, we are given glimpses of the entirety of God's universal plan. Heschel says, "God is not always silent, and man is not always blind. In every man's life, there are moments when there is a lifting of the veil at the horizon of the known, opening a sight of the eternal."

Burning

Even as our evolving consciousness permits us to pierce the veil and, now and then, become aware of some of the hidden secrets on the other side, dare we speculate on how our house burning down fits into the Divine plan?

Burning is not only a reality, it is a metaphor, a symbol.

Burning peels away, destroys what was; it begins a process of purification, rebirth, and renewal.

Burning requires "going through the fire" and being forged and strengthened in it.

During the last part of October and the first part of November 1996, not only Ellen and I and our neighbors, but many, many other people report "going through the fire."

Some actually experienced real fire as we did. In Oregon, the multiacre retreat center of a noted spiritual writer burned to the ground, and the New York apartment of the famed jazz musician Lionel Hampton burned just days before he was to receive the Presidential Medal.

Others were challenged physically and emotionally. In those weeks there seemed to be an overabundance of deaths, diagnoses of serious illness, lost jobs, broken relationships, conflicts among parents and children, colleagues, co-workers, and clients.

Was there some kind of "universal burning," a "universal purifying"?

Was there an end to old forms so that new forms might take their place?

Was the fire—and the related traumas—a message to me? to Ellen? to our community? to the world?

Were diverse soul contracts, and diverse soul missions, coming together to identify and play out a tiny little bit of God's grand universal plan?

Were we somehow being prepared for a different, a greater, role in the evolution of humanity, in the evolution of our planet?

We may never know the answers to any of these questions.

But the very fact that the questions arise may signal a subtle shift in human consciousness, a greater perception of what may be coming as part of God's ever-unfolding design.

Beyond Burning

Dare we speculate on how the pain and suffering we experience fits into God's grand design?

A pediatrician gives birth to a child with Tay-Sachs disease—an inherited genetic disease that always results in the death of the child by age five or six. In caring for her child, the doctor experiences a level of love that exceeds anything she ever felt before and that, surely, no one ever taught her in medical school.

For the rest of her career, she cares for her young patients with extraordinary compassion. And, of course, she makes sure that prospective mothers and fathers are pre-tested for Tay-Sachs disease so that the genetic defect will not be passed on, and that no other parent will have to suffer the kind of pain she so intimately knew.

Her own pain and sadness over the death of her child is always with her, but the doctor senses that her soul mission is to save lives that otherwise would have been lost and to bring compassionate love to the practice of medicine. And she understands the great gift her child gave her—even in five short years.

A "golden" young man—with incredible talent for academics, athletics, and music; with a sweet, charismatic personality; with wisdom beyond his years—contracts leukemia. The only possibility for saving his life is a bone marrow transplant. But no one in his family is a match, and, at the time, the National Bone Marrow Registry has fewer than 35,000 potential donors on record. Almost overnight the community comes to his aid: the call goes out for blood testing to find a potential marrow match; the media spreads the word; synagogues and churches open their doors as test sites; volunteers post flyers and make phone calls; large sums of money are raised to help pay for the tests.

After many months of waiting and hoping, a match is finally found. The transplant takes place; to prevent infection, the young man is kept in isolation for more than three months. The entire community rejoices at his progress; his big grin touches every heart. But, months later, his body begins to reject the transplanted bone marrow. Every medical treatment is tried; none works. At the age of fifteen, the young man dies. The entire community weeps.

His soul mission was short in earth terms, but, oh, how much he accomplished in his few years. In practical terms, his case helped make the entire country aware of the need for bone marrow donors. The National Registry now contains the blood test results of more than one million people. His mother went back to school to study grief therapy. With great understanding and empathy, she now counsels parents going through the agony she once experienced. On a soul level, this young man's deep wisdom and winning personality drew people toward him and drew people together. He taught people how to live—fully, richly, and nobly. He inspired people to share and to give and to love. He showed people what is important; he put life into perspective. It would have been good to have him on this earth for decades more, but in his short soul journey, he left an indelible imprint. He left a spirit that still hovers.

Three college students are driving down the highway when a car, driven by a drunk driver, swerves into their lane. In the head-on crash, one of the young men is killed; the two others suffer severe injuries and are in the hospital for months.

One of the survivors is so devastated over the loss of his friend, so angry at God for permitting the accident, so bitter over his own painful injuries, that he swears that he will never set foot in church again, that he will renounce God for the rest of his life.

The other survivor is touched by the visit of the hospital chaplain. He wonders why the chaplain would take such an interest in him—a total stranger. He begins talking with the chaplain about the accident, about his deep sadness at his friend's death, about his frustration in being cooped up in the hospital and his anger over missing a semester of school. He asks the chaplain for books to read about how other people endured pain and suffering, books about where God is when life hurts. With the chaplain, he begins to talk to God about his pain, about his sadness, about his anger and frustration. Slowly, slowly, he begins to hear God talk to him, and he takes comfort in God's love.

Months after he is released from the hospital, this young college student is still deeply affected by his friend's death and deeply bewildered about why such pain should befall him, but he is still in conversation with God. Slowly, his faith grows, and slowly, his life's path begins to emerge. After graduation, instead of enrolling in an MBA program as he had planned, he enrolls in seminary and studies to become a minister.

Decades later, after years of preaching and counseling and marrying and burying, after years of speaking with young people in hospitals—just as that chaplain had done with him—the minister comes to realize that he came to this earth with a soul contract to serve God by serving others. Had it not been for the accident, had it not been for his friend's death, had it not been for the pain he suffered, he might not have been led to faith, to God. But from out of his pain came

the recognition of his soul mission, and thousands have bene-
fited from his sacred ministry.

A fifty-three-year-old woman is enjoying life as the wife of a
successful businessman. Married right out of college, she
tended the house, reared the children, and hosted her husband's social events. Now she spends most of her time social-
izing with her friends at the country club. Once a week, she
volunteers two hours of her time to read to a blind woman in
a local nursing home.

One day, the dreaded phone call comes. Her husband has
dropped dead from a heart attack. After the initial shock
wears off, the woman is in a real quandary. In his will, her
husband has left her controlling interest in his company, but
she knows absolutely nothing about business or finance. Their
children, who live out of state, have their own careers and are
not interested in coming into the family business.

Her first thought is to sell the company, but, soon, the
woman sees it as a challenge—and a way to fill long, lonely
hours. She asks all the key associates in the company to teach
her the basics of the business. Slowly, slowly, she begins to get
involved in the operations, offering a suggestion here, taking
on a small task there. Over the months, she becomes more
and more familiar with the company and takes a more and
more active role. Eighteen months later, she asks the board of
directors to appoint her chief executive officer. There is much
doubt—and much consternation—among the board members, but, because she holds the controlling votes, she prevails.

Ten tears later, the company has flourished beyond anyone's wildest imagining. The company's earnings have
increased a hundredfold, and the woman is now a multi-
millionaire. She is incredibly pleased and deeply satisfied with

her performance, but she senses that something is missing from her life. One day, she remembers the old blind lady in the nursing home to whom she used to read. She calls the home to inquire about the woman, but, by this time, the woman has died. Not quite knowing why, she makes an appointment to visit the director of the home.

Touring the facility, she somehow feels as if she has come home. She immediately senses why she has become such a successful businesswoman. The great sums of money she has accumulated are not really hers; they belong to the most needing in her community. On that day, she writes a check to the home and soon becomes its largest contributor and greatest supporter. Over the next few months, she becomes aware of other great needs in her city—the food pantry, the homeless shelter, the AIDS clinic, the battered women's shelter. She opens her heart; she opens her checkbook. Before long, this woman is one of her city's greatest philanthropists. She introduces her friends to her causes and solicits their support. She uses her position as CEO of her company to encourage other companies to corporate giving. Her philanthropy spreads to other places in her state and, soon, all across the country. Because of this one woman, many of the downtrodden are lifted up, many of the hopeless are given hope.

She knew that "she always had it in her," but her early life and lifestyle never permitted it to show through. Though grief-stricken at the loss of her husband, confused and adrift, she became "her own woman." Because she was able to reach deep inside and find her soul mission, tens of thousands of lives have been enriched and ennobled.

A twenty-seven-year-old woman is jogging in the park when she is accosted, brutally beaten, and raped. Horrified by the at-

tack, and devastated by how she was violated, she is equally
stunned at the embarrassment of the police who took her report
and at the curt treatment she received at the hospital. She wonders if other women who are raped are treated in the same way.

Three years later, this woman has turned her outrage into
action. She has rallied friends and associates to her cause,
spearheaded the drive for funds, lobbied for the support
of government agencies. Today, she is presiding over the
dedication of the Rape Crisis Counseling Center at the
local hospital.

She is still feeling the effects of the assault; she is still afraid
of being alone for too long. But, she knows that there was a
reason for the trauma she experienced. It awakened in her a
sense of purpose, a sense of mission. She knows that she is
here in this lifetime to help care for and protect women—
women who are considered by many to be weak and vulnerable. She is to help her sisters claim their power and their
strength. Her body still hurts, her psyche still aches, but her
soul sings, because it has found its purpose and its mission.

A thirty-six-year-old man is a self-proclaimed "workaholic."
He works from dawn to midnight six days a week. On Sun-
days he works only until sometime around three or four in the
afternoon—unless, of course, there is a deadline or a crisis he
must attend to. He always reserves Sunday afternoons for
"family time" with his wife and three young children—unless,
of course, he is too exhausted. It's been this way for years, and
he really, really intends to stop one day, but, first, he wants to
build up the children's college fund, and then he wants to
make sure that he has set aside enough for retirement. And
even when there is more than enough money in the bank,
there is one more deal just around the corner. But, as soon as

he finishes that deal, he promises himself and his wife that he'll take it easy.

His first heart attack, at age forty-three, is just a "mild one." The doctor tells him to stay in bed for at least a month, and he fully intends to follow the doctor's advice, but there is a merger taking place in Paris. Even though he can't go, he sends two assistants and monitors their progress hourly with the cell phone and the fax machine that have been moved into his hospital room.

His second heart attack comes when he is forty-seven. This one is much more severe than the first, and he is in much more pain. But two weeks later, his secretary comes by with a set of papers that just can't wait any longer for his signature.

Just after his fifty-fourth birthday, his chest pains are so overpowering that he stops by the hospital for a "quick exam" on his way to a conference. Two hours later, he is in the operating room having quintuple bypass surgery. Although some permanent damage has been done to his heart muscle, the doctor expects that recovery will be fairly normal. But twelve hours later, the man suffers a massive stroke. The whole right side of his body is paralyzed.

For two days, his life hangs in the balance. Then his body begins the slow and painful healing process. But it isn't easy. He is slow of speech; he can hardly walk; he cannot use his right hand. Therapy helps; his wife and children are loving and supportive; his friends offer encouragement. But the man is deeply depressed. He cannot do business, so his reason for living seems gone; he can barely control his own body movements, so his way of living seems gone. He sinks deeper and deeper into depression; he is forlorn almost all the time.

One day a friend brings a canvas, a brush, and a set of paints to the man's house. "Here," she says, "why don't you try these?" The man just laughs. He can barely move his right hand. How would he ever be able to paint? Besides, he has no talent, no skill, at painting. The canvas and the paints gather dust in a corner.

A few months later, the man is at home by himself. He has seen every rerun on television at least a dozen times. He doesn't have the patience to read. All his friends are at work; they don't have time to visit right now. He is upset and uneasy. He just doesn't know what to do with himself. Then his eyes fall on the canvas and the paints. His left hand does not even know how to hold the brush, but he begins.

Fifteen years later, this man's paintings are displayed in galleries and museums and are part of private collections throughout all the world. His stunning art has brought great pleasure and much joy to hundreds of thousands of people.

Although some of his physical limitations have been improved through intensive therapy, he still paints with his left hand. The old workaholic is very reflective now. "I had no idea," he said, "that I had any artistic talent at all. My painting can't be anything else than the expression of my soul. Over and over again, the universe, or God, tried to tell me to slow down, to stop working so hard, to look inside and see what was there. But I never listened. I just kept working and working and working. Then, the universe hit me over the head one last time, and I had no choice but to listen. I lost my right hand, but I found my soul. And I guess that these paintings are my soul gift to me, and to you."

In the mid-1950s, a ten-year-old boy is on vacation with his family. They are driving from their midwestern home through the southern United States on their way to Florida. One afternoon, they stop at a roadside ice cream stand for refreshments.

Heading for the rest room, the boy sees two doors. The sign over one of the doors reads "Whites Only". The sign over the other door says "Negroes". The boy has never seen signs like this at home, so he asks his parents what they mean. His father gently explains the realities of the separation of the races in many southern states.

The young boy's sense of justice is deeply offended. Righteously indignant, he refuses to use that bathroom and refuses to order an ice cream cone.

Years later, that youngster becomes a political activist. He marches in civil rights demonstrations; he participates in a sit-in to help integrate a restaurant. He is in Washington, D.C., when Dr. Martin Luther King gives his "I Have a Dream" speech. After high school, he spends a summer registering voters in Alabama. After college, he goes to work for a civil rights organization. Later, he goes into politics and, eventually, is elected to the state legislature and then to Congress. He is a well-known and passionate human rights advocate; his entire life and career have been devoted to assuring equal rights for every human being.

In an interview, he was once asked, "How is it that you, a white man who grew up in the affluent suburbs, became such an activist for civil rights and human freedoms for blacks, for browns, for all minorities?" He thought for a long while before he answered. He told the story of coming to the roadside ice cream stand when he was ten years old. He said, "My soul was stirred. I simply could not abide those two signs. They offended every fiber of my being. From then on, I knew that I would spend my life getting rid of those signs and every bit of ignorance and hate they represent."

That man's soul told him early on what his life's mission would be. And rather than ignoring it, or fighting it, or running from it, he listened to his soul. He embraced his mission, and, because of his work, untold numbers of men and women of every color, race, religion, ethnicity, and creed have been given a taste of equality and human dignity.

Neither of them can understand what went wrong. They were high school sweethearts. They were so in love. Their marriage seemed so good.

But then, as the modern magazines so blithely put it, they just seemed to grow apart. They had different interests, different tastes. They drifted away from each other. He had an affair. He wasn't quite sure what he was looking for, but he didn't find it. When she learned of his affair, she had a brief fling with a friend at work. It didn't mean anything. It was just to prove to him that if he could do it, then she could too. They tried marriage counseling, but it didn't work. They were unhappy—deeply unhappy—but they didn't know why. They knew that their marriage was broken, but they just did not know how to fix it. Finally, because he couldn't take the uncertainty any longer, he moved out, rented a small apartment, got a lawyer, and, three weeks later, filed for divorce.

They were both miserable. She had never been alone before, and she was afraid. He hated staring at the four walls of the tiny apartment. They spoke on the phone once in a while, each hoping that they would find something—anything— that might draw them back together, but nothing ever did. Eventually, a year elapsed, and the divorce became final.

She is sure that she will be alone for the rest of her life. He is sure that no woman will ever find him attractive. Truth be told, they are both pretty miserable. As before, their lives just drift along, except that now they are alone and they have very few prospects for the future.

It would be nice to report that in a moment of revelation, they each saw their soul missions, realized that they were better off, and went on to fuller lives, better relationships, and greater happiness But that hasn't happened to either of them—yet. Perhaps it will—if they open their hearts and listen to their souls talk.

For waiting for them on the other side of grief and pain is soul mission and life purpose.

On the Other Side

When one gate swings shut for any of us—for all of us—there is always another gate waiting to be entered.

In the wake of the anguish of loss and the pain of suffering, there is always the hope of reconciliation and recovery.

There is always the possibility of new and deeper understanding, wider and richer perspective.

There is always the promise of evolution and growth.

That is why we can all come to understand and appreciate what the anonymous Confederate soldier knew so well.

> I asked God for strength
>> that I might achieve;
> I was made weak
>> that I might learn humbly to obey.
>
> I asked for health
>> that I might do greater things;
> I was given infirmity
>> that I might do better things.
>
> I asked for riches
>> that I might be happy;

I was given poverty
    that I might be wise.

I asked for power
    that I might have the praise of men;
I was given weakness
    that I might feel the need for God.

I asked for all things
    that I might enjoy life;
I was given life
    that I might enjoy all things.

I got nothing that I asked for,
    but everything I had hoped for.
Almost despite myself,
    my unspoken prayers were answered.
I am, among all,
    most richly blessed.

When we tame our suffering and grow through our grief, we come to Dr. Kübler-Ross's fifth and final stage of mourning: acceptance.

Our grief is transmuted.
Our lives are transformed.
We are wiser and stronger than ever before.

Continuing Creation

With the deep knowing of eternal souls that are partners with the Divine, we know that the act of creation is never over, for the very nature of creation is that it continually creates.

We know that old forms will surely shatter and that long-held certainties and long-felt comfort will be destroyed.

We know—and celebrate—the new light that brings new designs, new truths, new touchstones, new canons, new paradigms.

And we realize that nothing is ever the same.

For we—and everything with us—are growing and changing for ever and ever.

10

WHAT NOW?

"They" say that "time heals all wounds."

Don't let "them" fool you.

The raw grief and the searing pain may fade over time, but the sadness of loss and the empty place deep inside never fully go away.

For, despite our understanding of our soul's mission, we are still human beings with human emotions, human attachments, and human reactions.

My friend the doctor was right. After tragedy, my life—your life—will never be the same.

But God—and life itself—always offers the hope and the promise of healing, of renewal, of transformation, of growth, of new opportunity, of unending possibility, of newfound joy.

Soon after the fire, a number of my friends and colleagues reminded me of the story told about the great Chasidic rabbi Reb Levi Yitzchak of Berditchev.

Reb Levi Yitzchak taught that there are two kinds of sorrow and two kinds of joy.

When a person broods over the misfortunes that have come upon him, when he cowers in a corner and despairs of help, that is a bad kind of sorrow, of which it is said, "The Divine Presence does not dwell in a place of dejection."

The other kind of sorrow is the honest grief of a person who knows what she lacks.

The same is true of joy. She who is devoid of inner substance and, in the midst of empty pleasures, neither feels it nor tries to fill her lack, is a fool.

But the one who is truly joyful is like a man whose house has burned down, who feels his need deep in his soul and begins to build anew—over every stone that is laid, his heart rejoices.

I truly hope that Reb Levi Yitzchak was right.
I'll let you know.

BEYOND NOW

In the canyon were seeds that have lain dormant
for hundreds of years.

Only in the intense heat of the fire
could their shells crack open.

They have taken root and begun to grow.

From out of the inferno that destroyed so much
that was so precious,
new life
—never seen before in living memory—
has come.

And the landscape is forever changed.

As it is written:

God will come,
put us on the anvil,
fire up the forge,
and beat us and beat us,
until
brass
turns into
pure gold.

ACKNOWLEDGMENTS

I take great pleasure in extending deepest gratitude and most profound thanks to those whose influence is reflected in this work:

- Our parents, Hyman and Roberta Dosick and Clarence and Anna Kaufman; our sisters and their husbands, Karen and Michael, Terry and Gary, Norma and Michael, and Betty; and my son, Seth, whose abiding love sustains us.

- Karen J. Anxick, who manifested amazing courage and fortitude in the face of the flames and great friendship and devotion ever since.

- Our friends and neighbors—triumphant survivors, all—who have risen up from the ashes with tenacity, grace, and dignity.

- My rebbes and teachers who—from near and far—taught me that it is still possible to talk of—and to love—God even in this rational, scientific age: Rabbi Dr. Jakob J. Petuchowski ל"ז, Rabbi Shlomo Carlebach ל"ז, Rabbi Dr. Zalman Schachter-Shalomi, Rabbi Dr. Abra-

ham Joshua Heschel ל"ז, Elie Wiesel, and the Rev. James
J. O'Leary, S.J.

- My colleagues and friends whose wise counsel and soul-
  spirit helped shape this book by gently—but forcefully—
  harnessing my emotions and honing my thinking: Sandi
  Dolbee, Dr. Kathleen Dugan, Dr. Gary Hartman,
  Dr. Steven R. Helfgot, Rita Holm, Sherri Kaplan, the
  Rev. James J. O'Leary, S.J., Dr. Michael Meltzer, Rabbi
  Dr. David M. Posner, Rabbi Jack Riemer, Dr. Virginia
  Shabatay, Dr. Yehuda Shabatay, and Laura Walcher.

- The men and women whose words of blessing grace the
  covers of this book. They are all servants of the spirit,
  bringing new light to our complex and often troubled universe, and new hope and promise to our questing souls. I
  am greatly honored by their endorsement of my work.

- My cherished literary agent, Sandra Dijkstra, who con-
  ceived this book even while I was still standing in the
  ashes. From out of the chaos, she offered renewal, direction, and purpose. I shall be forever grateful.

- My esteemed editor John V. Loudon and the folks at
  Harper San Francisco, who demonstrated great faith in
  me and the book I could write—even when there was
  not yet a word on paper, because I did not have a piece of
  paper. As I wrote, John challenged and cajoled and dared
  me, and made me go to those deepest of places in the
  writer's soul. This book—and, I trust, I—is so much better for the journey. I am also very grateful to Karen
  Levine, John's most capable assistant, who most grace-
  fully shepherds my work through the maze of the publishing world.

- Most of all, I humbly and ever-gratefully offer never-ending thanks, boundless praise, and deepest love to Ellen. She is, in the words of the Proverbs (19:4), most simply and most profoundly, "a gift from God."

PERMISSIONS

Deepest thanks is expressed to these authors and publishers for permission to quote from copyrighted and original material.

Central Conference of American Rabbis for "Birth Is a Beginning" by Rabbi Alvin Fine, from *Gates of Repentance*, 1978.

DR. GARY HARTMAN for "A Psalm for the House."

The Prayer Book Press, Media Judaic, for materials from *Mahzor Hadash, The New Mahzor for Rosh HaShanah and Yom Kippur*, compiled and edited by Rabbi Sidney Greenberg and Rabbi Jonathan D. Levine, 1977 and 1978, including the works of Rabbi Sidney Greenberg.

Every effort has been made to identify copyright holders and obtain permission. Any omissions or errors will be most happily and gratefully corrected in the next edition of this work.